Thou Shall Be Happy:

*A Psychological Perspective on the 10 Commandments &
How They Can Help the Modern Person Find Happiness.*

By Dr. C.F. Martin

Contents

INTRODUCTION

I love flying. I especially love flying by myself when I don't have to talk to anyone or listen to anyone. I find flying alone to be such a great opportunity for peace and self-reflection. In our busy lives, opportunities for peace and reflection can sometimes seem hard to come by. Trust me I know! I am a mother of two wonderful children, and a wife to a chatty husband. I am also a psychologist, so I listen and talk to people professionally all the time! I love people, and I love great discussions, and I also love silence.

Being a mother of two, and a wife, and a psychologist, you can imagine that getting "alone time" for me is a challenge! So when my friend invited me to her baby shower in Texas, you can bet your bottom dollar that I went! I live in Arizona, so my friend's baby shower provided me with one of my favorite guilty pleasures- flying alone on a plane. The flight was magical. I got to read a book, I got to drink a mimosa, and I had a chance to drift off into the land of daydreams with reckless abandonment. It was everything I had hoped it would be! The baby shower was also fun!

On my glorious flight **alone** back to Arizona, an unexpected thought came to mind. Earlier that year, I had attended a Baptism Class at my church. In order to get my daughter baptized, I had to attend this one morning seminar on the meaning of baptism and the history behind it etc. While at the seminar, the presenter asked the class, "what was the Original Sin?" Almost in unison the class responded with, "Eating the Fruit from the Forbidden Tree."

To this the teacher responded, "Ah! That is what most people say! And yes that was the action of the sin! ...However, the crux of that action was the sin of Selfishness. She wanted the fruit. So she disregarded the agreed upon rules, used her free will, and acted in accordance with what she wanted. She acted selfishly."

At the time, I smiled and nodded- and agreed. What he said made sense, and then I moved on with my life. After that morning seminar I did not really give his insight into the Original Sin much thought. Not until I was alone on my flight back from Texas. While peacefully gazing out of the window at 30,000 feet I found myself thinking this:

"If the Original Sin was more about *selfishness*, than about disobedience or stealing, then what if all of the Comandments also had deeper messages than I had originally assumed. What if all of the Commandments had a deeper message that goes beyond the importance of our behaviors and civility, and are more about ways of finding peace and happiness? What if we have just missed them all these years?

Maybe then the 1st commandment isn't just about a need to believe in God, but is also about the importance of having

BELIEF and FAITH. Maybe the 3rd Commandment isn't demanding that we have to go to church every Sunday for our salvation, but rather that God wants us to live with integrity, and to act on our beliefs, whatever those are. While the straightforward takeaways from the Commandments are good rules to live by, what if they could be so much more? What if all of the Commandments were never intended to be strict rules of conduct? What if, instead the 10 Commandmnets were God's glorious and loving instructions for us to learn how to be happy?"

As soon as this thought was over I turned over my Southwest napkin and frantically started writing down all the Ten Commandments in a column labeled 1-10. Then I wrote a dash, and a blank line next to the possible alternative message that the particular commandment could have within it. By the time we touched down in Phoenix I had written the Skelton outline of this book.

The 2nd Commandment Controversy

This book will be following the St. Augustine version of the 10 Commandments. This version was chosen for no other reason than this was how I originally learned the 10 Commandments, and because I do not need Sister Elizabeth coming after me for participating in any deviations from her teaching! However, to be respectful and thorough, I will address the underlying message in the Protestant's 2nd Commandment of not worshiping false idols or images.

While forbidding the act of worshiping false idols is clear, the subtle message of how to live a happier life is to **not get attached to things**. Learning to let things go is an incredibly liberating experience. If you worship things, or are materialistic, you will never be happy. It will be a one-way relationship that will leave you feeling empty until you find something else to "worship" and adore for a while. If it was made by man, it can be destroyed by man. It is not special. You are special, way more special than any object on this Earth. *You* are the only irreplaceable thing on this Earth. Not your gold watch, not your car, not your boat, etc. Worshiping any item on earth is essentially beneath you. Don't do it. These are the types of messages that I will be extracting from each Commandment to help build your "toolbox" for building a happier life.

A Little About the Author's History

Watching a loved one struggle with a mental health condition is heartbreaking. It's like watching a person in a horror movie walk into the room where you know that the killer is hiding in the closet. You find yourself screaming at the TV, begging them not to go in, but nothing you do stops the person from entering the room and facing the dire consequences. The field of psychology has fascinated me for a long time now. While I grew up in a loving family, the issues of addiction and depression were introduced to me at a very young age. Without naming names, I have witnessed multiple different people in my life struggle with alcoholism, drug addiction, crippling anxiety, eating disorders and severe depression. Some overcame their inner demons, and others could not.

Watching a loved one struggle with a mental health condition is heartbreaking. I have been navigating the waters of mental illness in one way or another most of my life. While it certainly had its challenges, and I would not wish that experience on anyone, I believe being confronted with mental health issues early on molded me into the person I am today. It provided me the energy and motivation to learn as much as I could about psychology and mental health treatment. It also allowed me the personal growth opportunities to cultivate empathy and compassion for my clients, my client's family members, and all the others out there who struggle in silence with poor mental health issues.

I will never forget the moment I decided that I wanted to be a psychologist. I was 11. I asked my mom if we could go do something and she said that she couldn't because she was driving a family member to "the doctor." Here is essentially how the conversation went:

I said, "*The doctor? Is she sick? She doesn't look sick to me.*"

"Well, she isn't that kind of sick honey. She is going to a special doctor that... (um) helps people feel better about themselves," said my very kind mother.

"*Feel better about themselves? What does she have to feel bad about herself about. She is beautiful and popular, and has a car. What exactly does she have to feel upset about?*" – my eleven-year old self. To which my mother responded:

"Well honey. She doesn't see it that way. She doesn't see what you or I see. Sometimes, some people need help seeing those things, and this special doctor helps those people."

Later that day I found out that this "special doctor" was called a psychologist. I remember thinking about how great that doctor's job sounded. *"A job where you make people feel better? How amazing! How special! What a great way to earn a living."* While many of my childhood thoughts have changed- this one has not. Being a psychologist is great. It is amazing, and it is a great way to earn a living. I would just add that being a psychologist is also a privilege and an honor. To help people on their road to recovery, and to watch them climb out of their dark abyss and into the light is an amazing experience that some clients have been generous enough to let me be a part of. Poor mental health is dark, and it is dangerous, and it is also defeatable. While I do not always get the chance to know the outcome of all the different people that I counsel, I like to think that somewhere in my past, or even in my future, someone will remember me as the "special doctor" who helped them see how special they are.

If It's the Hard Thing To Do, Then it's Probably The Right Thing To Do

My childhood experiences fueled my passion in attempting to understand people and their behaviors which eventually inspired me to earn my BA in psychology. If my BA taught me anything, it was that I barely learned anything, and that if I wanted to further my understanding of people, I would have to get a doctorate in psychology. After years of graduate schools and poorly paid internships, I earned my PsyD in psychology and am now a clinical psychologist. Most people would say that it takes a lot of time and effort to become a clinical psychologist, and they are right. Getting a doctorate in any field is hard, but for me it was the right thing to do. That is usually the case by the way: If it is the hard thing to do, then it is probably the right thing to do.

Hard or not, I love my job. It's true. I love what I do. I consider it an honor to wake up every day and attempt to provide comfort and new perspectives to folks to help guide people to living a better version of their lives. If you have never seen a therapist, make an appointment today. You won't regret it. None of us are getting out of this thing called "life" unscathed, and a therapist is trained to help you work through things to live a healthier, more efficient, less stressed life.

All that said, in my practice, I have discovered that living a healthier happier life does not require any heavy lifting at all. Even after all the articles and books I have read; even with all the years of higher education and practicing psychology in vivo, I believe that the "secret" or "secrets" of living a healthier/ happier life are well within everyone's grasp. They also do not tend to be secrets at all.

Caveat: I'm a Psychologist, not a Theologian

I want to note before moving forward is that this book is not a theological discussion on the "true meaning" of the Commandments. The Commandments are The Commandments, and they should continue to be followed verbatim! I am not a theologian or Priest and I am not pretending to be one. While I went to Christian schools and was instructed in the Catholic faith, and while I do have a lifetime of experience of being in the Catholic Church, this book is by no means any attempt at fantasizing that I am some sort of expert on the Bible, Christianity, or any other faith.

This is also not a book on morality or how to live a more "Christian" life. Some of the things in here may even seem counter to a traditional "Christian lifestyle." I implore the reader to accept my apologies now if this is upsetting you! I am writing this book as a clinical psychologist who is attempting to connect the great wisdom within psychological research and the great wisdom from the Old Testament. While it may seem to some that these two schools of thought have little in common, I want to highlight how these two great sources of wisdom can help alleviate our day-to-day, self-imposed suffering.

Why I Decided To Write This Book

After my epiphany about the 10 Commandments on that fortuitous flight, I started researching how my 10 new interpretations could be helpful and applicable in everyday life. In my world, counselors call things that are helpful in stressful times "coping skills." It did not take long to recognize the connection of modern day coping skills to my 10 new interpretations that I pulled out of the 10 Commandments. For the most part, the coping skills I teach my clients are the same basic values that the Church (or any decent kindergarten) teaches us in our childhood. The problem is that no one talks about these basic values anymore. Some examples of the core concepts that I often impress upon and reacquaint my clients with are the things like Honesty, Kindness and Compassion.

I was taught these concepts in my childhood primarily through daily life with my family, and my weekly Sunday School. While my family and The Church taught me about worthwhile principles and values, like "Kindness" and "Honesty," I feel that society has progressed (or regressed) so far away from those values that we live in a world that has no time for those values anymore. This observation is something that makes me feel very sad. To make matters worse, I feel like even organized religions have become demonized and seen as "old fashioned" or boring, or even brainwashing factories. It is now seen as "weird" for a 20-something year old to attend Sunday Mass, while it is considered "cool" or normal for that same 20-something year old to get pregnant out of marriage, have a one-night stand, or be an addict. What is wrong with us?

Our values have been flipped. Modern society is so caught up in materialism, shamelessness, money, greed, self-promotion, and believe in the "dangers of organized religion," that I have observed basic values being hunted down to the point of extinction! They may as well be placed in a glass box in a museum somewhere in the space-time continuum. While we have made leaps and bounds in medicine and science, our communal morality has taken leaps and bounds backwards. My biggest fear right now for society is that we will figure out how to land a person on Mars before we can figure out how to be kind to each other right here on Earth.

I believe that if our society could wade backwards in time, to a period where we valued things like honesty and kindness, we would all be a healthier, happier and safer people. (I mean, there must be some truth in the saying, "The good ol' days!") Alas, we cannot go back in time, but it is still possible to resuscitate these forgotten virtues and bring them back to use in everyday life. And while we cannot make everyone follow these core values to create a perfect world, we can apply them to our lives and our world.

I also felt compelled to write this book because all the typical suggestions in my private therapy sessions and in this book are non-medication-based techniques that are free, and need no advanced training to perform. From a public health standpoint, I felt that it was my responsible to share these free, non-medicated ways of improving a person's mental health. To that extent, imagine how much better our communities would be, and how much safer they would be if everyone could achieve and maintain good mental health? It would be Utopia! Good mental health is within everyone's grasp! I truly believe this. I also believe that our God, our Great Spirit or Higher Power (whichever term you are comfortable with) wants us to be happy. I know some scholars disagree with my belief, and that's ok. It's *my* belief, and that is their belief, and this world is big enough for everyone to have their own beliefs.

Your Toolbox of Coping Strategies

The opportunities to be happy are there for you. Sometimes these "golden nugget" opportunities need to be dug out from the dirt, and other times they will present themselves as huge boulders! You just need to believe that you are worthy of happiness, and have the courage to seize it. You also have to have the courage to approach your old problems and issues with new skills and tools and to try to solve them again from a new angle, with the new tools. You can't build a house with just a saw! No matter how skilled you are with that saw, you will never build a house with just a saw. You need many tools for that, just like a person needs many tools for maintaining wellness. With that visual in your mind, I want you to imagine a person who uses one coping strategy for all their problems. Let's say that a person likes to "avoid" when they are stressed or depressed. Avoidance can be a great tool. Avoidance can provide us with a sense of safety, depending on what we are avoiding. At least for a while, avoidance will allow us to put that stressor on the back burner. Or take it off the burner all together! Stressed about talking to your ex-boyfriend at the high school reunion. Go ahead and avoid. No harm will come from not talking to someone you haven't talked to in 10 years. However, a person that only uses Avoidance for all their problems will also inevitably face more problems of a.) Never really solving a problem b.) Loneliness, c.) Continued anxiety; and D.) Depression about how the problem won't go away or change.

Building a repertoire of coping strategies is critical for living a happy life. I want to help you build up your toolbox. I understand that change can be scary, or hard, so we can go slowly. But even if it may sound hard, I encourage you to persist. If there is one thing I have learned, it is that if it's the hard thing to do, it's probably the right thing to do.

Is it hard to quit our addictions? Then it's probably the right thing to do. Is it hard to apologize when we have been in the wrong? Then it's probably the right thing to do. Is it hard to be polite? Then it's probably the right thing to do. I picked up this phrase from Dr. Najavits' book called <u>Seeking Safety</u> (2002.) It is a great manual for the treatment of post-traumatic stress disorder (PTSD) and substance abuse. Whether you specific struggle with PTSD, substance abuse, depression, or are just feeling stuck- this phrase will help you! I will be saying this phrase throughout the book so I encourage you to embrace it now! Let's say it again out loud, **"If it's the hard thing to do, then it's probably the right thing to do**." Without further ado, here are the "secret" lessons to happiness that I found in my interpretations of the 10 Commandments that I believe could guide us all to living a happier and healthier life. I hope you find them as helpful to your life, as I do in mine.

CHAPTER 1: "I am the Lord your God, you will have no other gods before me."
(The Secret- Believe in Something)

The exact intent of this commandment is clear- "I am your God- don't worship anybody or anything else but me!" The Bible sort of leads us to believe that God got angry and jealous about some people worshipping this golden calf statue, and so that is why this commandment was the first one. I interpret it as being the first one because Judaism needed to quash polytheism in order to become the dominate religion or at least the dominant religious style with monotheism. It is also a great introduction commandment. The reader needs to accept this commandment as true in order to respect and comply with all the other commandments. This commandment is saying- "HEY! I'm the one true God. Anything that you think you have heard about another "god" is false, and as such you do not need to follow anything they may have said. I am the only One, and therefore the only One that you need to listen to."

My heart always jumps a little whenever my depressed patients tell me that they have a faith system. Their faith makes my job that much easier. I don't need to try to sell them on ideas about "Fate" or how the universe strives for balance. While it is true that the universe strives for balance, a person believing in

God is alright at an advantage for improving their lives. Patients who have a belief in God are patients who are already meeting me half way on their road to recovery. This isn't to say that atheists are doomed for a life of depression, I'm just saying that individuals with a belief system already in place greatly helps.

When I say "belief system," I am including those who practice anywhere along the spectrum from a general spirituality to organized religions. If you believe in God, Allah, The Great Spirit, Buddha, Vishnu, a High Power, the Universe, to other smaller sects of traditional faiths that I am unaware of, then I am talking about you!

From a psychologist's perspective, the Biblical statement of the first Commandment gives the reader and follower structure, and a clear idea of who is in charge. People like structure. There is comfort and security in structure and people crave it on a very deep level. Since humans are social creatures, they also like to know who is in charge, or who is the "alpha." This commandment captures all of those subtle messages. From a writer's standpoint, and from a leadership standpoint, it is an excellent lead statement to capture the audience's attention and respect. Bravo Bible!

Believe In Something

The great coping skill I see in the first commandment is that it is talking about the importance of faith. The importance of **believing** in something greater than the all-powerful YOU. Sorry to burst anyone's bubble, but in order to be happy you can't just worship yourself- no matter how amazing you are. Dr. Obadiah Harris, a modern day philosopher, often discussed the need for us humans to release ourselves from our egos in order to progress and evolve. I 100% agree with this assessment. In my experience, outside of truly nefarious individuals, we really are our own worst enemy. If you can image a "Road to Happiness," we are both the person walking along the path, as well as the troll living under the bridge, sabotaging our attempts to reach happiness. We must release ourselves from our ego driven pride, and believe in something greater than ourselves if we want to be happy.

Narcissists

While believing in yourself seems like a safe bet, these bets have not been proven to save us from loneliness. Believing in ourselves is a good trait, but believing in a higher power is a better trait. We are only human, with human weaknesses and limitations. While we may have a touch of the divine within us, we are not fully divine. We are human, and subject to disease, death, and everything in between. Having faith in something more powerful than the human body is a better bet.

Remember Narcissus? He was a mythical Grecian man who fell in love with his reflection in a lake and ended up dying there from thirst and starvation because he never wanted to stop looking at himself. Ultimately, Narcissus never found love or acceptance. Narcissus had no friends, and no lovers, and rejected affection from others out of a belief that they were not good enough for him. He led a life of arrogance, loneliness, vanity, and isolation, which set him on a path for pain and death. Such will be the life and death of all narcissists.

In modern times psychologists used this myth to name the mental health condition of Narcissistic Personality Disorder (NPD). While not every jerk out there meets criteria for a true diagnosis of NPD, many could still be called sub-clinical narcissists. While being a narcissist may sound like a fun time, true narcissists have a very sad existence. According to the American Psychiatric Association (APA), narcissists are impaired in multiple different ways including: poor identity development, poor abilities for self-directed behaviors, poor abilities for empathy, and poor abilities for intimacy with others. In terms of poor intimacy skills, the APA's Diagnostic and Statistical Manual, 5th Edition, narcissist's relationships are "largely superficial and exist to serve self-esteem regulation; while mutuality constrained by little genuine interest in other's experiences and predominance of a need for personal gain." In other words: It is all about them.

As far as poor identity development, the APA states that narcissists have "excessive references to others for self-definition and self-esteem regulation and have exaggerated self-appraisal with vacillations between extremes." In other words, they don't know who they are, (or who they hate, or what they want).

Finally, and one of the sadder parts in my opinion, narcissists also have poor abilities for self-directed behavior, primarily because they have such a poor sense of identity. They don't know what they want. How can they make plans for things they want to do (self-directed behaviors), when they do not know themselves well enough to know what they want to do? The APA sums it up by saying "Goal setting (for narcissists) is based on gaining approval from others."

There are many other symptoms and issues for people with this serious disorder, and unless you are a licensed clinician, please don't go around "diagnosing" all your ex-boyfriends/girlfriends/ or bosses. I bring up the criteria for narcissism to highlight the dangers of living a life where you value your image more than anything else.

Ancient Warnings

The ancient Greeks knew the dangers that can come with narcissism and wrote a myth about it to warn future generations. And the writers of the Bible knew it too. While the Bible does not use the word narcissism, it does use a similar term called "insolent pride." Proverbs 21:24, *"Proud, Haughty, Scoffer are his names, who acts with insolent pride."* "Insolent pride" is the Bible's version of narcissism - and who was the first narcissist in the Bible? Satan, of course. One quote from the Bible that discusses the dangers of insolent pride comes from Habakkuk 2: 4-5.

[4] *"Behold, as for the proud one,*
His soul is not right within him;
But the righteous will live by his faith.

*5 " Furthermore, wine betrays the haughty man,
So that he does not stay at home.
He enlarges his appetite like Sheol,
And he is like death, never satisfied.
He also gathers to himself all nations
And collects to himself all peoples.*

This quote reminds us that narcissists, like Satan, are never happy. They are never satisfied because they always want more. "He is like death, never satisfied." Sounds like a pretty sad existence to me. Heed their warning. While the ancients warned people about the dangers of narcissism, and the Commandments say to believe in the one true God, what I read between the lines is the critical need of believing in something (loving something) greater than yourself, and to have faith in that something.

Believe in SOMETHING. That's it. Whether you believe in Jesus or Allah, or The Great Spirit, Nirvana (the place, not the band), Moses, etc.- **Believe** in something and your life will improve. Belief gives our lives structure and boundaries, and more importantly it gives our lives a purpose. Having a purpose in our lives is considered a major source of life satisfaction. Living a life of faith, from an established belief system will give your life an increased sense of purpose, meaning, and fulfillment. Additionally, researchers have found that spiritual people tend to be more gracious, more compassionate, and tend to have higher rates of self-esteem and optimism that people who are not spiritual. Spiritual people also tend to strive towards their own self-actualization (or potential) and live more meaningful lives.

Further research shows that spiritual people are more likely to do things like volunteer (which has been associated with reducing feelings of depression for decades), and donate to a cause they believe in- which is a great activity to aid in identity formation and helping us feel good about ourselves. Spiritual people also are much more likely to do things like pray and meditate, both are great coping skills for reducing stress.

The Power of Faith in Vivo

I had a wonderful client who struggles with alcohol most

of her life. By the time she was my client she was 20 years sober and seeing me for mild depression symptoms. One day I asked her how she got sober and stayed sober after all these years. She told me that she has been going to AA and doing the steps when she found out that her 3 year old grandson, and 1 year old granddaughter were put into Foster Care after my client's daughter was declared an unfit parent by the Department of Child Safety. My client went on to say that it was that moment that she realized that her new sober life was meant for her to be able to take care of her grandkids. She thanked God for her sobriety, and for her new PURPOSE in life. She reflected that if it was not for that moment and those kids and her belief in God that she doesn't know if she would be alive today. My client would tell you that God saved her. I would tell you that it was her faith in God and her new purpose that saved her. This is a perfect example of how having a belief in something IS a coping skill.

The Secret Coping Skill: Believe

Believe in God, or the Universe, or something else that is greater than yourself. You cannot be your own God. You cannot be your sun and the planet- you cannot rotate around yourself! This commandment is asking you to believe in, have faith in, love and value something beyond yourself. Research has shown that religion and spirituality are generally associated with better mental health and tend to have a positive influence on patients' overall quality of life. One study from 2010 measuring the effects of religiosity on health and well-being found that "people who identify as religious tend to report better health and happiness, regardless of religious affiliation, religious activities, work and family, social support, or financial status," (Green & Elliott, 2010.) Another study from Weber & Pargament (2014) reported that, "Greater religion or spirituality has been associated with: lower levels of depressive symptoms, fewer symptoms of posttraumatic stress, fewer eating disorder symptoms, fewer negative symptoms of schizophrenia, less perceived stress, lower risk of suicide, and less personality disorder." This study also concluded that religion or spirituality has been shown to act as a protective factor with greater adherence to psychiatric treatment.

Find a religion, or some set of religious beliefs to serve and follow faithfully. If you haven't found it yet, that's ok! The road is long and there is still time to find it. Volunteer, research different religions, attend different churches, pray on it, meditate on, etc. If you hate God, or the universe for some tragedy, learn to forgive God for all the struggles you may have surpassed. Your anger and resentment for God will only hurt you. While your love for God will only serve you. Do whatever it is you need to do to find your higher power to believe in. It is out there. Life becomes a whole lot easier, clearer, and impassioned when we can wake up with a purpose, or a goal, because of our belief systems. The Japanese even have their own word to describe this idea. They call it, "ikigai," and it means, "*a reason for being.*" The Japanese people believe that uncovering their individual "ikigai" is important in life because finding it will opens the doors for a person to have satisfaction and meaning.

The consequence of not finding meaning will be a life filled with loneliness, self-pity, and depression. Religion and faith give our lives a needed sense of purpose, as well as a better sense of control in this otherwise crazy, unpredictable world. With faith, all things are possible. With faith, all suffering has meaning. Without faith, the world remains a dark and scary place full of painful, meaningless suffering. Come out of the darkness, and believe. If you haven't found a faith that you can connect to, keep searching. The pursuit of faith is a worthwhile endeavor.

Practical Ways of Applying Faith & Belief as a Coping Skill

In addition to research and theory, I want to give some very concrete ways of applying this skill in everyday life. As you think more about this skill, I am sure you will come up with other ways of applying this skill in your own unique way. To start, here are some quick ideas as to how to apply Faith and Belief.

- Pray. Pray every day, at least once a day. It can be a formal prayer, or something you made up. It doesn't matter, as long as you are praying to a Higher Power that is all that matters.

- Meditate. Try taking three minutes out of your day to meditate and connect with your thoughts. One of the goals of meditation, outside of obtaining a feeling of peace, is to reach a higher level of awareness, and thus increase our connection with our environment and the world at large.
- Spend time in Nature. Nature is a great visual reminder of the power and beauty of the world. Allow yourself to relish in it, and think about how nature was created.
- Research any old and new religions. Read books on the topics, meet with religious leaders, take a class on it at your local college. If you have not connected with any organized religions that it fine, but the journey through education is always productive.
- Exercise hope and reduce control issues. You can't expect yourself to know everything. Work on any anxieties and control issues that you may have, in order to tolerate the unknown. When we release ourselves from control, we can receive hope
- Avoid Cynicism. Cynical views and statements are at the opposite end of the spectrum of belief and faith. A cynic's doubt and suspicion will only bring anger and hopelessness.

CHAPTER 2: "I am the Lord your God, thou shall not take my name in vain."

(The Secret: Kind Language)

When I first learned this Commandment in my childhood, I thought it was because God wanted us to respect Him. Again, this rule makes sense. For the Commandments to work, God needed us to respect Him. Today, it means something far deeper and more intimate to me. While preparing the first draft of this book, the basic coping skill for this commandment came very easily. The unwritten lesson here is to use *kind language* with ourselves and with others- at all times. This is a concept I discuss almost daily in my private practice. I cannot promote it enough.

Some people believe they find strength in profanity and speaking down to others. But the crux of those behaviors are both driven by anger and fear. Not a lot of good things tend to come from anger and fear. With either of those emotions, individuals tend to lash out, and make rash, impulsive decisions that tend not to end well. And while the initial feelings of power from unkind language may feel good in the moment, that moment will be short lived, and that angry person will be left with only the memory of how they were made to feel less than, disrespected, or afraid. Additionally these angry people typically have a surge of guilt from whatever mean things they said, or they have a lot of needed apologizing to do in order to repair that damages that their anger caused.

Basic Instincts

I would like you to ask yourself, "What do most animals do right before they strike out when they are afraid or angry?" What does that animal look like to you?" Once you have a visual, I want you to ask yourself, "Does this animal look happy or at peace?" No! They look terrifying! They bark or growl or make some sort of aggressive sound. Some animals can even make their fur stick out to make themselves look bigger. I was once chased by an angry goose at the park. It was terrifying! I accidently walked too close to her nest and she attacked! Mrs. Goose lowered her neck and stretched out her wings and charged right at me! I ran for my life! Mrs. Goose was angry, and I was terrified! Neither of us were at peace.

Humans forget that we are not that much different from the other animals on this planet. Replace the word "animals" with "humans" in the first sentence of this section, and it could still be read the same. "What do most *humans* do right before they strike out when they are afraid or angry?" Hopefully a human won't growl but, a human will typically start broadening their shoulders, standing taller and or slinging out vulgarity, or other negative comments. When we humans feel threatened (physically or otherwise), something is signaled deep within our brains that queues up what I like to call our "survival switch." (This is more commonly called the Fight or Flight system that lives in our sympathetic nervous system.) This switch essentially makes us more animal and less human. What I mean by this is that this switch allows us to harness our deeply embedded survival skills that us "civilized" humans do not normally have to exercise. Fight or Flight mode allows us to care more about surviving rather than what social etiquette would require. We become "feelers" verses "thinkers," and this can be a very dangerous switch to make. When the choice comes down to civility and/ or survival, we are going to choose survival every time. To survive is instinctual, but it can also be ruthless. This is one reason why rescuing a drowning person can be so dangerous. They are in such a panic to survive, that they won't even realize that they have you by a strangle hold and are pulling you down with them.

The human brain is capable of making quick, smart decisions, and it is capable of making long term and short term plans and seeing both the short term and long term consequences of our behaviors. But when we get scared, some of our exceptional human brain skills get thrown out of the window. This is why in the movies, the terrified girl runs up the stairs instead of more wisely running out the door. This is why panicked people run into the streets and get hit by cars. They are so focused on trying to survive that they lose focus on how to stay alive.

Unlike the movies, most of us are not being chased by serial killers on a regular basis. Therefore more typical triggers for the average person include a.) Being late to work, b.) A fight with their spouse, or c.) Bills. Notice that none of these things can actually kill you. An envelope notifying you that you are late will literally not kill you. Your wife yelling at you for drinking too much will not kill you, and being late to work will not kill you. No one has ever been admitted to the ER for the above issues. No mortician ever wrote: "cause of death: bad hair day."

The Pen Is Mightier Than The Sword

While the above is all true, our brains have come to associate everyday stressors as threats that need to be taken care of swiftly! We have come to associate common annoyances as being threats to our integrity or our lifestyle. We see all these triggers as threats, and we know that brute force will not solve these problems, so we turn to our other set of weapons- our words. Remember the quote, *"The pen is mightier than the sword"*? This quote is just as true and just as applicable today. If a sword, or another weapon will not be effective, let's use our words. Using our words as weapons is seen in the News, politics, and gossip columns every day! The Bible even discusses the same idea in Proverbs 18:21,

" Life and death are in the power of the tongue."

With a simple movement of our breath and tongue, we can either lift ourselves up to the light of hope and joy, or we can thrust ourselves into the darkness of hopelessness and fear. We can make people believe a falsehood, or we can inform them of our truth. It is our choice how we want to be effective, and our speech is an incredible weapon. Why else would the first Amendment of the United States be freedom of speech? Our Founding Fathers knew how powerful language was, and other nations know this as well. Silencing a people is the first step towards their disarmament.

Words matter. Semantics matter. A person who dismisses or minimizes the importance of word choices and semantics will more than likely have chronic communication problems. To accurately understand ourselves and each other, we need to exercise accurate language. Words can be such an incredible force. From speeches that inspire nations, to poems and lyrics that cause us to cry and reminisce about the past, to the stand-up comedians that have us holding our stomachs as we "belly laugh" so hard it hurts, to the horrible break-up letter your ex left on your kitchen table- words are incredibly powerful. Use with caution. Once you say something you can never take it back.

Slinging out insults is easy, and it can make us think that we are hurting a person who hurt us. The desire to hurt someone who hurt us is understandable. It is not a very mature or evolved thinking process, but understandable. As a general rule, seeking tit-for-tat justice will typically leave you feeling unfulfilled. This is true in death penalty cases for murder and it is true in your everyday life. When someone hurts us, and we want to hurt them back, it is important to recognize that hurting them will only make you feel *justified*, not necessarily *happy*. If someone keys your car, and you key their car back, do you now feel happier? I doubt it. While you may have felt powerful, or justified or maybe even vindicated by keying the other person's car, I doubt there was any happiness there. After you return to your car, you still have to process and deal with your own keyed car, and not to mention any lingering feelings of being disrespectful or victimized by someone. I implore you to really begin to identity your emotions. Feeling *powerful*, feeling *vindicated*, are not the same feelings as feeling *happy*.

The Power of Kind Language

Another logistical problem with "unkind" language to others is that it typically shuts down the opportunity for civil mediation or any platform for explanations. While passion is typically the catalyst for fights, com-passion is typically the solution. Mean language and vulgarity quashes that option. When individuals lose chances or opportunities to explain themselves or find out more about the issue at hand, people can start making up the other person's intentions in order to fill in the gaps. This is a serious problem. Believing that you KNOW the intentions of another person is a true delusion. Unless you know some secret way of practicing telepathy that I am unaware of, you do not know what others are thinking. This type of arrogance is murderous.

Humans cannot read minds, and choosing to believe that another person's intentions and motivations were nefarious will only make you feel worse. If you have a tendency to believe that people's intentions are always bad or aggressive, start challenging yourself on the evidence for that belief. Put on your white lab coat, and start asking for objective proof for your assumptions. Become a critical thinker, not just a critical speaker.

The Truth Doesn't Matter

Let me give you another example. Let's say you are driving along, minding your own business when someone speeds up beside you, cuts you off forcing you to slam on your brakes, only for the other driver to get into the other lane and fly off. No wave, no nothing!

A very typical (and understandable) thought you may have

23

from that experience is "That asshole cut me off!" While the action/verb part is true- "cut me off," the subject of "asshole" implies that the person is a mean, bad person, and the implied message is that he did it to you personally. (After living in LA for a year, I had this experience MANY times.)

Let's work backwards and first tackle the implied message- *that he did it to you personally.* Trust me, that LA driver would not have cared if it was you or not. He would not have cared if the person in your car in that specific location and time was you, the Pope, or the President. That driver felt compelled to get over into your lane and so he did. It wasn't about you in the least. Secondly, and to my point on kind language, it is overreaching to assume he is an "asshole." To label someone as anything is an all-encompassing description of that human being. Maybe the driver is actually a good person who just didn't see you. Maybe the driver is actually a good person and just got news that his family member just got sent to the hospital or that his home just got broken into? Now are you starting to feel more compassion for this driver? Would it make you feel better to believe these thing vs the original beliefs that he is an asshole? I think so. Here is the important part: We will never know the truth. You and I will never "get down to the bottom" of the mystery of whether the driver is a good or bad person, or why he cut you off rather than someone else. Especially if you live in LA, or another big city, you will probably never see him again. The truth is, that the truth doesn't matter. *What matters, is what you choose to believe.*

Releasing yourself from the negative thoughts about this stranger and his actions will also release you from feeling assaulted, threatened or otherwise disrespected. Embrace that you cannot give yourself "the truth." This will then make it easier to allow yourself to create an alternative interpretation of the actions that occurred. Then, sense you are already making things us, why not create something nicer and kinder to believe that will make you feel happier?

We also direct negative comments and beliefs to ourselves all the time. We drop a glass and it shatters all over the place:

"Damn it! I am such an idiot!" While no one likes to break things, it happens. We are not robots, so we are going to make mistakes sometimes, and mess up. No big deal- it's a glass. Yelling at yourself will not make the mess go away. It will only send you deeper into the self-loathing abyss, making it much harder to climb out of. We miss out on little opportunities for self-compassion all the time. Self-Compassion, through acts like kind language is the yellow brick road to happiness.

Seize Opportunities to be Happy

Every day we are faced with hundreds of opportunities to be kind to ourselves. Happy people seize these opportunities for kindness, while unhappy people seize every opportunity they can to cement their beliefs that they are worthless, stupid, ugly, unlikeable people. If we already have a fixed belief that we are stupid, worthless, ugly, etc., it is easier and oddly more comfortable to accept this as the status quo. It takes courage to challenge our beliefs. Change is hard, and can typically be scary. Learning to look in the mirror and see a decent, smart, kind human being can be a difficult task for some people who have learned to look in the mirror and see an indecent, stupid, spiteful human being. The war of identity politics we wage in my minds is merciless. But remember what I say, "If it's the hard thing to do, it's probably the right thing to do." Learning to be kind to yourself will be one of the most important things to ever learn to do for yourself.

The Secret Coping Skill: Kind Language

If you have that critical/ mean tendency of viewing yourself and others in a negative way, I am challenging you to start using kind language for a month starting right now. I promise you will not regret it. This exercise is free and is a non-medicated approach to mood management. No vulgarity, no cynicism, no negativity, just compassionate kind language to yourself and others for a month. (And if you really want to say something mean, find a more intelligent, tactful way of insulting someone. At least put some effort and creativity into your habit of breaking down people. Winston Churchill once said, "tact is the ability to tell someone to go to Hell in such a way that they look forward to the trip." Tact does make insults more challenging and impressive when you succeed, but seriously if you find yourself REALLY wanting to say something mean to someone or about someone, just don't say anything at all. The world will keep spinning without everyone else knowing your thoughts and options.

Once we can reduce our tendency of feeling threatened and disrespected all the time, it can become much easier to use kinder language! If we can increase the threshold to our survival switch, we can remain calmer, more collected, and more thoughtful people capable of producing kind language. As with the driving in LA example, when we can remain calm in the face of unwelcome events such as getting cut off, we can respond more as thinking humans, versus feeling animals. A thinking human can respond by noting, "Oh wow he is going fast," (an observation) or "Oh wow that was close!"(a slightly subjective observation) or even a "Wow he must be in a hurry," (a positive assumption about the other person's behaviors.)

Responding calmly to unwelcome situations will maintain your emotional stability and ultimately your life satisfaction. Negativity is an airborne disease. Whether you are breathing out negativity about yourself or others, or you are breathing it in from another person spewing negativity in your vicinity, you are either going to infect those around you, or you will keep yourself sick because of the negativity that you are breathing in. One great thing about being your own problem, is that you can then be your own solution!

The Secret: Kind Language Continued

Negative words and negative talk also tend to serve as platforms for people you are talking to, to also complain about anything. For example, if you have ever started a conversation with, "You know what I hate..."? A typical response is "I know! You know what else I hate?" And before you know it, you and your talking partner have complained about several different things, and none of those things have changed, and neither of you feel better about the situation. Misery may love company, but she hates solutions, and resolutions. While it may feel good to "let off some steam" about a topic" that feeling will be short lived, and the insidious nature of negativity will creep back over you until you are as unhappy about something as you ever were. If negativity is the disease, kind language is the cure.

If you want to be happy, use kind language with yourself, and with others. Using kind language will produce more positive feelings. The more positive feelings we have, the more likely we will feel happier more of the time. So what if you screwed up at work? "Whoops." Remind yourself that we all make mistakes, and that you will try not to do it again. Not only will you feel better handling the mistake this way, but you will also have just saved yourself probably 30 minutes of your work day since you didn't go hide in the bathroom and berate yourself about what an awful worthless employee you are. Making a mistake does not make you a worthless employee. Hiding in the bathroom for 30 minutes- **that** makes you far more worthless of an employee. Get back to your office, own the mistake, correct it, and move on with your life. Not only did you fix the mistake, but you also gave yourself something to feel proud about, which will be another positive experience for the day.

So what if your son failed his math test? Calling him stupid or a failure will only make him feel worse, and will keep you angry. Talking to him and offering compassion will inspire him and keep him in a place of safety so that he can perform. I was seeing this young patient for several years before he was college bound. He was very sweet, and suffered with extreme anxiety. Among other things, he was a victim of severe emotional abuse with a foundation of cruel, unsupportive language. He shared with me that one of his biggest fears of college was failing a class, because then that would "prove" that his father was right about him being an "idiot" and that he will never succeed. In that moment, I could have chosen a variety of very traditional psychotherapy routes of challenging his cognitive distortions or "All or Nothing Thinking", and trying to expand his view of success and failure, or developing more coping skills to tolerate negative emotions and experiences such as failure. All of those routes would have been sound therapy. However, I took a leap of faith and instead I exercised Honesty, self-disclosure, with the intent of instilling more compassion and kind language self-talk.

I said, "John, what would you say if I told you that I failed two classes in college?" When I told him this, his jaw dropped and he said, "No way. You're like a nerdy doctor." I said, "Yes I am a doctor. I am a doctor that failed two classes in undergrad, and a class in graduate school. I had to retake all the failed classes, which I passed on the second try, and then just kept going." I explained how I made some mistakes, which I suffered conse-quences for, and that I made up for it and kept marching on. After I shared what I physically did, I highlighted how I was able to use kind language as a coping skill for allowing me to reach my goal-which was to graduate. I explained how I chose to see that the grades were a reflection of my mistakes and that they were not a reflection of my global skill, or that they were a reflection of my fate. I used positive, kind self-talk to say things like, "You will get it next time," to keep my going. John is currently a junior in col-lege and doing well.

Sticking with kindness will keep the negativity at bay so you can practice kind language and stay solution focused rather than problem focused. Instead of, "You are such an idiot! What is so fricking hard about algebra?!" how about, "Honey, a lot of kids struggle with math, how can I help you?" Compassionate talk, kind language, will always open the door for a more positive so-lution focused conversation. It also provides an opportunity to nurture a relationship with the person you are talking to. Kind talk provides the platform for a happier life.

The Power of Compassion

If you are looking to feel powerful, try being vulnerable. What takes real strength is the courage to be vulnerable enough in the first place to talk things out as mature human beings, and the humility to know that you don't know everything. You feel threatened or hurt in some way? Tell the person, and have a con-versation about it. Keep your human brain! Keep your humanity!

The Dalai Lama XIV once said,

"If you want others to be happy, practice compassion. If you want to be happy, practice compassion."

In my experience, these are very true words. This can all start through kind language. The words we use becomes our inner narrative and also becomes our lens through which we see the world. When we start using kind language with others, we will naturally start using kind language in our self-dialogue, and before you know you will start believing that little voice in your head. It goes back to that old saying, "if you don't have anything nice to say, don't say anything at all." This is good advice in your communications with others and with yourself. Life will present enough obstacles in your way; don't let your own language be one of those obstacles.

Change Your Narrative

If your inner narrative says that you suck and that you will never accomplish anything, then you have already lost the race. If you tell yourself that you are stupid and ugly, and you value intelligence and beauty, you will never be happy. It is not hard to say to yourself, "I am a worthy, beautiful and priceless person." It costs you nothing to say to yourself, "I am awesome and loveable." The side effects of practicing kind language to yourself will be an increased sense of self-esteem, and quality of life. The cost of not practicing kind language will be continued pain, self-doubt, fear and self-loathing. Kind language may be one of the single best things you do for yourself this year. While I am not your therapist, let me help you start this kind language exercise. These are exercises I give to my patients every day. Every morning, wake up and say to yourself, "I've got this," and every night before you go to bed, tell yourself, "You did great." Replace absolute terms with less severe words. This turns phrases from, "I'll never succeed" into "I'll get it next time." And with that mindset you will!

Practical Ways of Applying Kind Language as a Coping Skill

Kind Language is a wonderful gift to give yourself. Below is a list of practical was of applying Kind Language to your everyday life:

- Notice your negative words. They may seem automatic. In fact, a lot of therapists even call them "ANTS- Automatic Negative Thoughts!" Noticing that we have a problem is the first part of solving any problem.
- Replace and Rephrase. Whenever we notice that we used a negative/harsh word, just go back and replace it with a more positive/less critical word, and give it new phrasing. This is very similar to learning a foreign language. This will take training but it is easy and pain-free. For example, the next time you make a mistake a work and call yourself an "idiot," I challenge you to calm yourself down, and Replace and Rephrase. So then you would say to yourself, "I'm not an idiot, I just made a mistake."
- Stop Using Absolute and Catastrophic Language. Stop saying phrases like "FML." This is doing you nothing but bringing you down! Stop using incorrect, dramatic language that fuels feelings of depression. Stop saying things like, "Worse Day Ever," "It was a total disaster," or "I look like a cow." The Chernobyl Nuclear Power Plant explosion was a disaster. September 11, 2001 was the worse day on American soil ever. Cows look like Cows. Stop using inaccurate dramatic language. This will only make you feel bad.
- Use Positive Affirmations as much as possible. Put up inspiration quotes around your room, or place Post-It notes in high visual places with kind statements to yourself. The more exposure to positive language the better. Put yourself in an Immersion Language Program for Kind Language. It is the most useful language in the

world.

- Speak no Evil, See no Evil, Hear no Evil. With the same idea of the Positive Language Immersion Program, reduce or eliminate as much negative content as possible. Don't watch programs with a lot of violence or cruelty. Don't expose yourself to people to speak to you with cruelty. Surround yourself with as much positive content as possible. I way that I did this was that I replaced a lot of suspenseful shows with travel shows. The travel shows I watch are always beautiful, positive, as well as educational!

- Watch out for Shoulds. To bring humor, and a visual into session, some therapists like to say to their clients "Stop Should-ing all over yourself." "Shoulds" have a very negative assessment of ourselves that lack compassion. Our *shoulds* tell us that who we are, what we are doing isn't good enough. *Shoulds* brew negative evaluation and keep us feeling down. To use Kind Language with *shoulds*, add on a kind/compassionate phrase like, "but I trying," or "and I am going to do ____ to make up for it." For example, "I should be making more money by now... but I am in school so I can get the degree I need to make more money.

- The benefit of the doubt. Give yourself and others the benefit of the doubt more often. This goes back to a theory in psychology called the Attribution Bias. This theory has been studied for over half a century now, with lots of research supporting the idea that our thoughts and our beliefs lead us to feeling certain ways! So rather than making up a negative thought about a person, without much evidence, go ahead and say something kind. If you don't know the truth about another person, why not make up something that will make you feel good rather than bad? This is one trick that happy people do. They choose to believe something positive, over searching for reasons to assume the worst in a person, themselves or the situation.

CHAPTER 3 - "I am the Lord your God, thou shall keep holy the Sabbath."

(The Secret: Act on Your Beliefs)

ACT on your beliefs! This one is simple. Even the original language of the 3rd Commandment is basically saying, "If you believe in Me, show Me that you believe in Me by worshipping Me on the Sabbath." Words and beliefs mean little unless you follow them up with actions. This is why I loving nicknamed this commandment, the "Show Me" commandment!

Being an "armchair activist" is not good enough. Talking the talk, without walking the walk will bring you no joy, and it will ultimately make you feel worse about yourself. You will feel worse because you aren't acting in accordance with your beliefs. "I 'liked' the Facebook page for the Wildlife Foundation!" Congratulations- you have accomplished nothing. Saying things means very little. Saying things like, "I am totally going to start working out tomorrow," and "I am quitting smoking" does nothing for you. Exercising and quitting smoking actually do things for you. Talking about doing things does nothing. Trust me, I wish it did. I wish I could talk about how well I am going to eat and how much I am going to exercise in order for me to reach my goal weight. I wished it worked that way- but it doesn't. Wishing and hoping for things doesn't get things done - doing things gets things done. And doing takes ACTION!

If I want to believe that you are a good parent, then you need to do good parent-like things. This may include actions such as: buying them books and toys, giving hugs and kisses, and providing emotional support and praise. If you believe that you are a good parent, and you do all those things, it confirms your belief that you are a good parent. This belief that you are a good parent, supported by your observable actions of what makes a good parent good, makes you feel good about myself, and so you continue to do good parent-like things to further reinforce the belief that you are a good parent, and thus the cycle continues. In this example, "Being a good parent" has become part of your identity, and as such it is something that has become integrated into how you see yourself.

Identity Formation

Erik Erikson, a forefather of Developmental Psychology, would call these individuals "identity achieved." Individuals who are "identity achieved" have "explored their options and developed a coherent sense of identity and are more socially mature and motivated to achieve than their peers. (Wenar & Kerig, 2006.)

Problems (depression/disappointment/shame/anxiety), or general stress arises when we behave in ways that are incongruent to our chosen identity. Ever done something that you feel guilty about? Here's why: you knowingly violated your own code of integrity. You disregarded your own, self-made code of ethics and beliefs. For example, if I see myself as a good parent, only to scream at the kids an hour later for something minor, then my ACTIONS have put into question my "good parent" identity. If I see myself as an environmentalist and as someone who cares for the environment, but then I litter, then my actions are incongruent with my beliefs again.

Who Are You?

"So how can I believe something about myself when I behave in *ways that are opposite to my beliefs about myself? It just doesn't make sense!"* Most humans do not like things that do not make sense, and we also do not like our identity to be questioned. For if we are not who we think we are...then who are we? *"Who am I?!"* This existential question is a very uncomfortable question for people to answer. Sometimes it is uncomfortable because maybe we really are trying to be something (a good parent, an environmentalist, sober etc.) and it's just really hard for whatever reason. In this case, people whose actions are incongruent with their beliefs will feel shame, guilt, etc. because their actions violated their own code of integrity.

Other times when people who are confronted with the "who am I" question become very angry because they don't know who they are, or what they stand for, are totally lost, and feel embarrassed about not knowing. For these people who are not so tightly connected to their labels, when they are called out that their beliefs don't match their actions, they will typically get more defensive and irritable. This is usually out of embarrassment because the truth is they do not know who they are, or what they believe, and they attached themselves to some identity or label because it was someone else's idea, or because it was the popular thing to do. They did not adopt the label because they truly believed in it. Essentially these people are the sheep of the world, and they are still looking for something to believe in-something or someone to follow.

The Dangers of Not Knowing Who You Are

When a person fails to connect to an identity, developmental psychologist believe that they can become "developmentally delayed." This essentially means that their psychological development, maturity, and or evolution is currently being halted. *"Youths who are confused and uncertain about their identity and are making no progress towards establishing one are termed "identity diffuse," and tend to be socially isolated, unmotivated and attracted to substance abuse (Wenar & Kerig, 2006.)"* Developmental psychologist also identity a similar group of people as "Identity Foreclosed." These individuals *have* declared a loyal identity to something that they have not really explored thoroughly, and also have not explored other options either. Outside of not knowing who they are or what they want, individuals here are also at a greater risk of becoming victims to things like cults or other extremist type organizations. *"Research shows that foreclosed individuals are rigid and authoritarian in their attitudes"* (Wenar & Kerig, 2006.) Being a rigid thinker with an authoritarian attitude is a sad existence, and an unhappy one to boot. Because their identities are so poorly constructed, sadly they need to be rigid and unbending in order to keep their identities from falling apart. Their identities are so fragile and poorly put together, that they always need to be on the defensive in order for their sense of self to not be shattered by the recognition that they have no idea who they are. The world is a scary enough place full of unknowns and mysteries. Now imagine how much scarier the world is when they wake up to discover that they not only know nothing about the world, but they also know nothing about themselves. When individuals here even get a sliver of awareness that they are wrong in some way, defensives go up, and they find a way to dismiss or invalidate the contradicting evidence. This action is both self-protecting as well as self-sabotaging at the same time.

(Footnote: Just to be thorough, developmental psychologists also have a term for people who have not made an identity but are actively engaging in exploring who they are- it is called Moratorium, and these people may have some anxiety about their situation but otherwise are in a good place with high-levels of self-esteem.)

Know Thyself

During sessions I always encourage my clients to get to know themselves! You have a lifetime to do it, and don't let that opportunity get away from you. You take yourself everywhere you go, and it will be the only thing you get to take with you into death. Getting to know yourself will be one of the greatest gifts you can give to yourself. I highly recommend this endeavor. Don't be afraid of who is waiting for you at the end of this journey. Whoever he or she is, is already alive and well living in secrecy inside your heart. Open your heart, and love and accept and embrace yourself. Get to know the inner you, and you will get to know you.

Whatever you believe in, whatever you say you love, follow it up with actions! Good intentions are "nice" but "nice" doesn't put food on the table or provide protection from the elements or enemies. "Nice" is never good enough for the long-term. Here are some examples that highlight how "nice" intentions are never good enough:

1.) "I totally meant to recycle that, but I didn't see a recycle bin anywhere and I didn't just want to carry it around with me all day, so I just threw it out in a regular trashcan."
2.) "I am totally opposed to eating veal. But it was all they had on the menu so I ate it."
3.) "I really was planning on getting sober today but then my boss yelled at me so I ended up drinking again after work.

Intentions are a nice start, but they are worthless in the Life Satisfaction and Love Department. If you say you love someone or something, show them the sacrifice. Love is sacrifice. If you can't sacrifice your own wants and desires for someone, then you don't love them. Period. You don't. No matter how much you think you love your wife, family, blah blah blah, at the end of the day your ACTIONS speak to what really matters to you.

The Secret Coping Skill: Act on Your Beliefs
So if you hold onto that grimy empty plastic bottle until you find a recycle bin- Bravo. That small sacrifice demonstrates your true beliefs on things like the environment or the community. If you are really opposed to the abusive treatment of calves, don't eat veal- make that small sacrifice. I have been told that veal is "amazing," but to stand by my own personal beliefs about the treatment of calves, I choose to make the small sacrifice of not eating something "amazing" in order to demonstrate me

beliefs. I live in America. A country with literally hundreds of eating options. I am not going to starve from this "sacrifice."

And if you are an alcoholic who says that you really love your family, you will get sober and you will make all the sacrifices requested of you until you reach that goal- or you will die trying- because that is sacrifice. That is love. Love requires sacrifice, and the ability to sacrifice takes love. And "sacrifice" is an action word.

One thing I often say in my individual session is this: "*Those who refuse to sacrifice anything will inevitably lose everything*." No matter what you want in life, no matter what goals you have for yourself. It is going to require some amount of sacrifice on your part. Whether the sacrifice will be your time, money, food preferences, energy, vulnerability, honesty etc. The universe is not just going to hand out lollipops for free. If you want to get something, you are going to have to sacrifice something for it. Your body likes balance, your check-book likes balance, and the universe likes balance as well.

Sacrifice in Action: Lauren

I had this lovely client once. Let's call her Lauren. Lauren was in multiple casual relationships, had what she called an "ok" job that barely paid the bills, and she was also obese. Lauren said that she wanted to be married and have children, and get a job that paid well, and be fit. While this next part was uncomfortable for me, as her therapist, I sacrificed my comfort in an attempt to help her reach her goals. I highlighted how her actions were not in line with any of things she said she wanted or believed in. In short, I pointed out that the reason why she wasn't getting any closer to her goals was because she was refusing to sacrifice anything for the goals she said she wanted. She said she wanted to be fit, but continued to eat unhealthy foods, and wouldn't commit to exercising on a schedule. I pointed out that she said she wanted a committed monogamous relationship with a man who loved her, but was continuing to have sex with multiple men that she would find on "hook-up" apps. Lauren also said she wanted a better job, but didn't want to spend the time looking for other jobs or go back to school to get the degree she needed to get the jobs that she wanted.

After a thorough analysis of her resources, we reviewed what she would feel comfortable sacrificing in order to make strides towards her goals. Lauren is now single, finishing up her first semester in college and is turning down dates with men who "just want a hook-up." Lauren sacrificed money and time, to hopefully gain a higher paying job in the future that will pay her bills. Lauren also sacrificed the pleasures of frequent sex and attention from multiple relationships, in order to devote more time into finding and nurturing a relationship with a man who also wants a committed monogamous relationship with the prospects of children. Because of sacrifice, Lauren is now two steps closer to her relationship and career goals.

Sacrifice

When we believe in something, sacrifice becomes easy. And when we love something, we come to a place where we don't even see it as sacrifice anymore, it just becomes the thing that we need to do, and it also becomes the thing that we want to do. It is no longer a burden. Individuals start to see "sacrifice" as the thing that we *get to do* in order to achieve our goals. "Keeping Holy the Sabbath" day is asking for believers to just do the things they say they believe in. It is the "show me" commandment. If you believe in Christ, pray to Him, participate in Christian holidays, and follow His teachings. If you believe in the United States, stand up for Her values and Her way of life. Vote, participate in a march, write to your senator, fly an American flag in your yard! If you believe in Muhammad, pray to the East and follow His set of values and code of ethics. Do whatever it is you need to do to prove to yourself and the world that you mean whatever it is you say you believe in.

One of my favorite quotes from a saint is from St. Francis of Assisi: "Preach constantly, use words when necessary." This quote is about action, and how our actions speak louder than anything we can say. When you do this, it will reinforce your belief that you are what you think you are. Acting this way will make you feel good about yourself because you would be acting congruently to your beliefs and self-image. No need to feel confused, or lost or guilty. You are who you think you are. If you like this identity you will find peace. If you don't like it- do something about it.

Practical Ways of Applying "Act On Your Beliefs" as a Coping Skill

Acting On your Beliefs is a great way of living a meaningful life, and a life that brings us happiness. Below is a list of practical was of applying this skill to your everyday life:

- Say what you mean, and mean what you say. Even with our words, it is important to be truthful and congruent. Don't tell someone you care about the environment when you don't. If you do care about the environment, tell people that you care about it with pride. Be courageous enough to be honest and stand behind your beliefs.

- Follow through on Promises and Commitments. Even when it is hard or inconvenient. Be dependable to your family, friends, job and community. Get to work on time, watch your son's basketball game, help clean up your local park. If you signed up for it. If you promises someone something, follow through.

- Evaluate and Challenge your Beliefs from time to time. As humans we do grow up and mature and evolve. Sometimes our beliefs can come with us, and sometimes we out grow them. Either one is one. Just don't fall asleep at the wheel. This exercise can also reinforce our beliefs and our commitments to those beliefs.

CHAPTER 4 - Honor thy Mother and Father.

(The Secret: Respect Others)

My parents used to love reminding me about this one. They used to jokingly call it "the most important commandment!" I had a very wise Sunday School teacher and he also taught us that this Commandment went both ways, and that parents are also expected to honor and respect their children! After all children are blessings and therefore should be valued as such. I used to love reminded my parents about that perspective as my rebuttal to their comments!

When I think about the words "Honor your mother and father," I instantly get an image of these well-behaved, well-mannered children who follow all instructions with a bow and a smile. This doesn't sound like such a horrible thing does it? Some children may ask questions like, "Why should we obey our parents?" Other than, "God commands it," or "because it pleases the Lord," there is one glaring reason to me as to why one should follow this commandment as is: 1.) Parents and other authority figures typically have decades more life experience, education, and thus typically has a much greater capacity for compassion than a child has. Adults therefore are more than likely in the better position to offer both guidance and safety opportunities for a child. 2.) Learning how to respect our parents will teach children how to respect others and ourselves as well. This skill will set up children for success in their careers, relationships, and life in general in any civilized society. If you ever want to be in a healthy relationship, and have a family, and a stable job, and not be imprisoned, then learning early on how to respect your elders and other authority figures is an essential skill to master.

The Importance of Family

I can remember the day when I learned that this Commandment went both ways: that children should respect their parents and that parents should also honor and respect their children. Those two rules gave me a visual of loving and giving parents who are kind and gentle with their children, and sweet children who are kind and respectful to their parents. What a wonderful place a family and a home could be if we all followed this commandment exactly as it is written.

As a therapist, (and as a person with my eyes and ears open) I am all too aware that this is not always the case. I hear and see and read about more children getting out of control, assaulting their parents, and disrespecting their teachers and elders, and communities in general. I hear about all forms of child abuse and cruelty, abandonment, and then I see those children struggling to figure it all out on their own. These lost children find communities in things like gangs and cults, and becoming more and more angry, and violent. This reality is in juxtaposition to what the original commandment wanted us to visualize. As a society, we never needed to understand this commandment better. As a society, if we want our civilization to survive, we need to save and honor the traditional notion of Family.

The negative impact of child abuse, domestic violence, trauma, parental abandonment, foster care, divorce, and growing up fatherless are too lengthy for the purposes of this book. So much sadness and pain is caused by all the aforementioned issues. The two issues that I will touch on in this chapter will be on Fatherlessness, and child abuse.

Fatherlessness

Fatherlessness is a real big problem in America right now, and it is a problem that is under researched and underappreciated for how impactful it is on a child. The National Fatherhood Initiative (2017), reported that 1 in 4 children in America currently live without a father. These children are four times as likely to be impoverished, seven times more likely to become pregnant as a teen, two times more likely to die in infancy, two times as likely to drop out of high school, and more likely to commit a crime, go to prison and have substance abuse issues. Additionally, the Department of Health and Human Services reported, "Children living in female-headed households with no spouse present have a poverty rate of 47.6%. This is four times the rate of children living in married couple families," (2012). Outside of poverty, and other heath factors that are increased (like obesity) children who grow up in father-absent homes are 279% more likely to carry guns and deal drugs than peers living with their fathers (National Fatherhood Initiative, 7th edition, 2015.) The long and the short of it is, kids without dads have a tough road. Never underestimate the role of the father. The commandment was right, children should "Honor thy Father." Concurrently, adult men and women need to honor the role of the father. Our children and our society will continue to suffer until we do this.

Child Abuse

Children with a history of child abuse are at a greater risk for a slew of problems ranging from poor physical health, injuries, increased risk of chronic health conditions, chronic mental health conditions like Borderline Personality disorder, Bipolar disorder, depression, anxiety, substance abuse issues, and incarceration.

In one study performed by the National Survey of Child and Adolescent Well-Being (NSCAW) on child abuse, they found that 28% of children with a history of abuse had a chronic health condition (Child Welfare Information Gateway, 2013). Another study utilizing a trauma questionnaire known as the ACE (Adverse Childhood Experiences) found that 58% of suicide attempts in women were connected to an adverse childhood experience.

The ACE questionnaire is a simple 10 question document

that asks a participant to answer yes or no to 10 different experiences. A person gets one point for every "yes," and zero points for a "no." ACE researchers have found that individuals with scores of 4 or higher are at a 1000% greater risk for developing chronic health problems. Individuals with ACE scores of 4 and higher are also seven times as likely to become alcoholics, twice as likely to get cancer, and 12 times more likely to have attempted suicide (Aces Too High.) The physical and psychological warfare that abuse and trauma wreak on a person's mind are unparalleled. Something else to keep in mind is the amount of money abuse and trauma cost taxpayers and the community. The financial burden placed on society from child abuse is astounding, and is something that I think most people forget about. "The lifetime cost of child maltreatment and related fatalities in 1 year totals $124 billion," according to a study funded by the CDC. Again, if we want to save our society, we have to save the Family.

The Dangers of NOT Respecting Others

Just to drive this point home, let's picture a child who struggles with abuse at home. He grows up with poor self-esteem, no healthy role models, and performs poorly in school. His drive to succeed is stifled, and maybe he turns to drugs and alcohol for comfort, and gets in frequent fights with others. He will eventually drop out of school, and struggle to find a job, until he gives up and turns to welfare. After decades of drinking, he now has a host of medical problems that the state now has to pay for. He is also at a community mental health facility for his depression, which is also being paid for by the state. This little boy, who was never respected by his parents, never learned how to respect himself or others, and now is 40 years old living off the state, and he too is now neglecting his own children, if he even knows they exist. This picture also did not add in the cost of the possible domestic violence calls the police had to take care of. Maybe this boy had to be sent to Foster Care, and Child Protection Services had to be brought in, with therapists or occupational therapists, etc. All of this pain and suffering and money could have all been spared if his parents just could have loved him more than they loved themselves.

I cannot write enough about how terrible the short term and long term effects of child abuse are. If I could wave a magic wand and end one thing on this planet it would be child abuse. Patience and compassion cost nothing, and those are two main ingredients needed to stop child abuse. The abuse needs to end.

The Secret Coping Skill: Respect Others

At its core, this commandment is telling us to **Respect people**! The word *respect* is translated from the Greek word *timēsate*, meaning "honor or value." When one takes the literal translation, *respecting* something ultimately means to "place a great value or high price on something." So when I say, "RESPECT PEOPLE" I am telling you to "VALUE PEOPLE." Value a person over your time, money, or reputation. Value a person's life and family and efforts over your car, time, or your other material possessions. That is respect.

Now that the word respect has been defined as "valuing people," I believe that this secret is really easy to apply. Basically, don't be a jerk. Be respectful and nice to other human beings, especially your family members. I have seen animals treated better than people and it is tragically sad. Respect takes minimal effort, and it will maximize your experience of positive feelings and emotions. Due to what is called the Cognitive Triangle, when can either manipulate, or be manipulated by our feelings. The Cognitive Triangle is a psychological construct that consists of three factors: Thoughts, Feelings and Behaviors/Actions, and they are intricately and automatically connected. The moment we do a conscious *behavior*, we will subsequently have a connected *thought* and *feeling* with that behavior. The moment you have a *feeling*, experience an emotion, you will subsequent *thought* and *behavior*; and likewise when you have a *thought* you will subsequently have a connected *feeling* and *behavior* from it. Because of this Cognitive Triangle, when we do *Behaviors* like, "respect our neighbor," this will immediately make us both *Think* things like, "wow I am a nice guy," or "that was nice," and *Feel* emotions like, pride, or happiness. Or when you *think*, "I am a respectful person," you will more than likely experience positive feelings, and behave respectfully. This cycle is always operating. Now that you have been introduced to it, I challenge you all to closely monitor your Cognitive Triangle, and practice more respect and see how it makes you think, feel, and behave.

Respect In Action

Be respectful, especially to your family. In my clinical experience, no worse psychological harm can be committed than when a trusted family member harms one of their own. Being betrayed by a trusted family member makes a person feel unvalued, and betraying a trusted family member will also make you feel bad about yourself. So don't do it! Respect your parents, respect your children, respect your elders, community members, etc. If you are struggling with respecting someone, than at least do no harm, and say nothing, do nothing. Remember, while doing nothing might seem like it is the less harmful approach, it doesn't necessarily make it the "right" approach. Because if it's the hard thing to do, it's typically the right thing to do. Likewise, it it's the easy thing to do, it is probably the wrong thing to do.

While ignoring is not kind, if that is the best you can afford in that moment, it is still better than a rude, nasty comment or physical assault. If you can increase respect for others, it will model for yourself and others how to be respected as well and thus increase your own self-respect because you are now acting like a respectable human being. It makes it harder to respect yourself when you are screaming at others and engaging in disrespectful behaviors.

Examples of respecting others in the Bible are everywhere. Jesus respected the prostitutes (Luke, 7: 36-50), David respected Saul (1 Samuel 24: 8-10), and the lions respected the lambs on Noah's Arc. When you respect others, you subsequently become more respectable to yourself and others.

Dare to Dream

Like all the other suggestions and tips in this book, practicing respect for others and yourself is a non-medicated approach to improving your personal levels of happiness and life satisfaction. When we die we cannot take with us our relationships, our money, or any of our awards. One of the few things that can last beyond our frail human bodies is our reputation. It is up to you to be remembered either notoriously, honorably or not at all. May we all choose to try to be remembered as respectable human beings, who respected others. May we all strive to be such respectful human beings that one day parents want to name their children after us! There is a reason why there are a million people in the world named "Jesus" out there and not one person named "Satan." Prophet or Son of God, Jesus is believed by most of the world that he was at the very least, a respectful human being who preached about the importance of love, and the importance of respecting each other. Dare to imagine how much better the world would be if we could all follow such a simple idea.

Practical Ways of Applying "Respecting Others" as a Coping Skill

Respecting Others is a great way of living a happier life. Below is a list of practical was of applying this skill to your everyday life:

- Respect your parents, respect your kids, respect that stranger on the street, respect your neighbor and your neighbor's kids etc. Disrespecting others will bring you no joy, while respecting others will increase your own levels of self-respect and pride. Try not to yell, scream, or demean others. Do not abuse others.
- Respect your body and your spirit. Eat well. Go to that doctors appointment. Speak kindly to yourself. Take vitamins, drink water, and wear sunscreen! Buckle up!
- Treat others like you would want to be treated. "The Golden Rule."
- Increase patience.
- Don't be violent. Don't be violent to yourself, to others, or to the environment. Also don't vandalize

property. Don't be violent with your actions or your words. "If you can't say something nice don't say anything at all."

- Don't lie. Be respectful enough to be truthful.
- Don't gossip.
- Stop speeding. Respect others enough to let them make it to your jobs and their homes safety. Respect pedestrians, and cyclist enough so that they make it home safely. They are all human beings. Respect them.

CHAPTER 5: Thou Shall Not Kill.

(The Secret: Honor Life)

"Don't Kill." While a general rule of "not killing people" seems obvious for a society to function, the greater life benefit of *not killing* someone making us happier may not seem as obvious. (Since this is not a legal or moral book, I am going to skip over the obvious reasons why murder is both typically seen as illegal and/or morally wrong. This book is designed to highlight how these "rules" have underlying life lessons to help us all live happier lives.) That being said, a good general life rule to follow is to still try your best not to kill others.

The coping skill that I pull from this commandment is the importance and value of **Honoring Life** as a precious, unique, and irreplaceable element on the Earth. If a person can honor life, and honor all living things, that person will lead a happier life. This concept of honoring life goes a little deeper than the skill of respecting and valuing life.

The task of Honoring Life generalizes to all living things, from humans, to wildlife, to the trees. Life is an incredible thing. Scientists cannot even bring conclusive data as to how it started, and personally I find the concepts of "instincts" as mind-blowing. What do you mean I am born knowing how to grasp and drink milk??? What do you mean some animals "know" to cling to their mothers??? When you really start thinking about it, life (in all of its forms) is truly amazing.

This concept never hit me harder than when I became pregnant with my first child. I got one of those Pregnancy Day-by-Day books, and between the photos and learning about what was going on in my body, I was awestruck by the power of nature and life. Then in addition to my already reverent attitude towards life, I learned something new about the human body towards the end of my pregnancy. When I was about 30 weeks into my pregnancy, I asked my OBGYN, "What starts labor?" I was expecting a response about weight or pressure on the uterus, or that some hormone is excreted...No. Instead she said, "No one really knows." Then when I finally got to hold my first child for the first time I became completely aware of why they call existence "the miracle of life," because it is. If you have ever had the privilege of holding a newborn baby in your arms, it becomes exceedingly clear how special and miraculous life is, and how natural it feels to protect that life.

I noticed that after becoming a mother, I became especially sensitive to news reports and TV and movie scenes that showed murder. I was struck by how fragile our bodies are. I wondered "how many people are grieving right now because of this person's death that is being broadcasted for all to see?" I became plagued with thoughts of, "Who the hell do these people think they are, taking another person's life just like that?" One bullet and the person is gone, and a family is destroyed. In one second that precious life that was brought into this world is gone forever. It was at this point that I started driving slower. It was also at this point that I started saying really nerdy things like "Arrive Alive" to myself and others! It was also at this point that I also started to save spiders and bees rather that smacking them down. I know I may have gone overboard but I felt good about it! The way I see it is this: Honoring life comes down to this simple rule: don't break something you can't fix or replace- and no one can fix or replace a life.

Murder and Mental Illness

The Center for Disease Control (CDC) estimated in 2014 that about 43 people are murdered every day in the U.S. (Kochanek, K., Murphy, S. L., Xu, J., & Tejada-Vera, B., 2016). In 2016, the FBI reported that there were 15,696 murders in 2015 (Crimes in the United States, 2015, www.fbi.gov/news.) Roughly the same daily numbers were reported by the CDC in 2011. Some of the murders were gang-related murders, drug cartel, planned assassinations, mass homicides, and "crimes of passion." A murderer could give many answers as to why they committed murder. "Gang initiation," "He had been abusing me," "I was fighting for my life," "It was war," "I caught them in bed together." The list could go on forever. For the purposes of this book, the bigger question that needs to be asked is, "Do you think these murderers are happy people?" To quote the great Elle Woods, "Happy people just don't shoot their husbands!" Truer words have never been said.

"They Must Be Crazy"

I believe there is a myth out there that people believe that all criminals are "crazy." First of all, this belief begs the question of what does "crazy" even mean? What does "normal" mean? Is a person "crazy" for stealing bread because they are hungry? Is a person "normal" for forgiving a murderer? These terms are laced with personal values and innuendos, and are hard to define. I personally think the myth that criminals are all "crazy" is perpetuated by a human need to separate "normal/good" people from "crazy/bad" people: "Oh they were crazy! I'm glad they are locked up now! Now I am safe!" Another reason I think we want to think that criminals are crazy is just because it is uncomfortable to even start trying to think like a criminal. Because of the discomfort, I think most people chose to abandon the exercise and just conclude that criminals do criminal activity because *clearly* they are just crazy and mentally ill. Again, what does "crazy" mean?

Researchers disagree about the exact percentage of murderers with a history of mental illness. Some conclude that it is as low as 10%, some say it as high as 19% (Torrey, 2011; Matejkow-ski, et al., 2008.) The Bureau of Justice Statistics reported in 2017 that among their prison inmates, 14% met the threshold for having serious psychological distress (Bronson, J & Berzofsky, 2017.) The Treatment Advocacy Center agreed with the lower range saying that "U.S. and international to date research suggests that individuals with schizophrenia and Bipolar Disorder (two serious mental health disorders) are responsible for approximately 10% of homicides in the U.S." Lastly, in August 2019, the American Psychiatric Association came out with this statement about murder and mental illness: "It is important to note that the overwhelming majority of people with mental illness are not violent and are far more likely to be victims of violent crime than perpetrators of violence."

In the March 2011 edition of the American Journal of Psychiatry, Dr. Torrey published his finding that "individuals with severe and untreated psychiatric disorders are responsible for approximately 10% of the **homicides** in the United States." Ten percent is not that high. Even 19% is not that high. That means that 90% to 81% of homicides are committed by individuals *without* a documented severe mental health disorder! Notice that I said, DOCUMENTED SEVERE MENTAL HEALTH DISORDER. Right now, I know that there are millions of folks suffering from some sort of grief, trauma, depression, anxiety, stress, substance abuse issue etc and are not seeking help for it. Instead, they suffer in silence and isolation, which only exacerbates their symptoms. Some people go to one psychotherapy session and never come back. Some are given medications, which they never take. This list can go on, but to be short and to the point- trying to identify and treat individuals with mental illness can be very challenging.

Aside from individuals with true antisocial personality disorder (which makes up 3% of the male population/1% of the female population) psychopaths, narcissists, or brainwashed cult/gang members and terrorists, I don't believe that most criminals look forward to a life of crime. I think most "criminals" have had a lot of poor role models, trauma, unstable attachment styles, or have experienced some level of pain and stress in their lives and chose selfishness and their survival above other people. But that is just what I think.

Again, I say this to eat away at the myth that all violent criminals must be crazy! They are not. Not all of them anyways. Individuals with mental health issues, documented or not, are typically suffering greatly, and are challenged with issues like poor self-esteem, lethargy, suicidal thoughts, panic attacks, anhedonia, lack of drive, hopelessness, and insomnia, to name just a few issues. To give you an example I will tell you about Peter.

Peter was a good guy who drank too much. He got three D.U.I. tickets in his early 20's, and as a result he served some time behind bars. He later lost his license after the third ticket. By the time I saw him he was in his early 30's, and he was presenting to me for issues with panic attacks. He was now sober, married, had 3 kids and a stable job. He shared that all the attacks happened when he was driving his car, or was getting ready to drive. We worked on coping skills for panic, and explored any traumas around driving. He denied any car accidents, or traumas with cars, but he neglected to share with me anything about the loss of his drivers license. He also never shared that after he got out of jail, he missed a court appearance. After about six months into consistent counseling, he finally shared with me his story of lossing his drivers license after his third DUI ticket, as well as the fact that he had an active warrant out for him from years earlier due to not appearing in court. Therefore, he knew that every day when he drove to work he was at risk for getting pulled over and arrested. He said he never shared it before because he doesn't like to talk about it.

Three months later he was pulled over for a broken taillight. During this time, the police officer discovered that he was driving without a license, and that he had a warrant out for his arrest due to not appearing in court for another traffic related issue. Peter said that he was facing months in jail for his crime of not appearing in court years earlier. As one can imagine, his panic symptoms spiked, and he was calling me a lot for support. Long story short he was sent to court about a month later. Peter did show up, and the Judge dropped all charges. He was now a free man.

Peter went on to say that he had been worried about getting pulled over for a decade. He shared that he knew he wasn't supposed to be driving, but that he needed to drive in order to work and support his family. So he decided to take the risk and drive, but he always drove the speed limit, and was always a very cautious driver. He shared that when he drove he was constantly looking in his rearview mirror for police cars, and refused to play music in the car because he thought it was too distracting. Peter suffered his anxieties for a decade, and it probably would have been longer had he not gotten pulled over. Peter is a perfect example of a "criminal," who was causing far more harm to himself than he was to society.

Individuals suffering from the aforementioned symptoms are not likely to break into your home or cause any violence! That would involve way too much energy. However, individuals suffering from mental health problems such as, substance abuse problems, anger management issues, impulsivity issues, poor processing skills, poor future planning skills, low empathy for others, and command hallucinations- now these symptoms could be dangerous. The combination of symptoms like these can be very dangerous, and I'm guessing this is where that 10% comes from.

But saying that "murders all have mental health problems" is both false and ignorant. Murder is certainly, extreme, and perhaps desperate, but not necessarily a sign of "crazy." So while the connection between documented clinically poor mental health and criminal behavior is there, it is also important to recognize that about 90% of homicides are committed by people with no history of mental health issues.

No Diagnosis Does Not Equal Being Well

However, just because it's not documented, or "not meeting criteria for diagnosis" does not mean that these people are happy go-lucky folks skipping through life. I would venture to guess that those 90% of murderers without a documented mental health history have a very long, unfortunate story to tell. They are not content, they are not satisfied. They are not individuals at peace with themselves or the world. I would guess that if you were to interview a random murderer, the odds will be high that this person is probably struggling with some sort of depression, anxiety, trauma or substance abuse issue either in their past or present. I have worked with several different individuals who have committed murder. They were all far from happy, and they were riddled with some or all of the above mentioned issues. Trust me, they did not show up in my office to tell me about their adventures in prison, or about the day they killed someone. For those who are interested, most of my previously incarcerated clients talk about their early childhood abuse or neglect, early exposure to violence through witnessing domestic violence between their parents, or some other traumatic experience with violence. Most also talk a lot about their relentlessly intrusive thoughts about their traumas, the murder itself, and or the violence they experienced in prison. Prison is a tough place to live.

Warning!

The therapist in me is compelled to say this next part: If you ever find yourself so angry and upset that you are actually thinking about killing someone- talk to someone. A friend, your partner, a therapist, the police! Seek help! You can save the other person's life, and you may very well have saved your own life by finally getting the help you need for any untreated anger management issues, mood disorder issues, or impulse control problems. Help is out there. Violence only breeds more violence. And killing your wife's lover will not make the pain of her infidelity go away. While passion starts most conflicts, com-passion is typically the greater force to resolve those conflicts. Killing that other person will only make your life more difficult. Between the possible trauma of watching a person die at your hands, dying yourself, and/or then the subsequent prison sentence or life as a fugitive is not fun, and will bring you no peace.

The First Murder

Let's reflect on the first-ever murder, the murder of Abel by his brother Cain. The story of Cain and Abel come to us from Genesis. The Bible does not go into much details about Cain's motives, but it leads us all to believe that Cain murdered his brother Abel out of jealousy.

Genesis 4: 3-5, "³And it happened in the course of time that Cain brought from the fruit of the soil an offering to the Lord. ⁴And Abel too had brought from the choice firstlings of his flock, and the Lord regarded Abel and his offering ⁵but did not regard Cain and his offering. And Cain was very incensed, and his face fell."

It was soon after this that Genesis reveals that Cain leads his brother into the fields where he murderers him. What happens next is the interesting part. God does not punish Cain with death for his crime. Instead, God "curses" him. ¹¹And so, cursed shall you be by the soil that gaped with its mouth to take your brother's blood from your hand. ¹²If you till the soil, it will no longer give you strength. **A restless wanderer shall you be on the earth."** (Genesis 4: 11-12.) Additionally, God "marks" Cain to scare off anyone that may kill Cain and take him out of his misery. I find this decision to not kill Cain for his crime, to be a huge act of compassion, as well an example of how to act with mercy in the face of a huge injustice. While the topic of capital punishment is hotly debated, and very political, I believe that this is very telling that God chose life over death in that decision. He chose to honor life, regardless of the sin. While the sentence of banishment is a huge punishment- Cain still got to live. He lived with the burden of both the guilt of his crime, and his punishment for the rest of his life. But he got to live. God still honored Cain's life, to show that life is something that needs to be honored.

Honor Life

Respect and honor life at all costs. This path will always bring you peace and self-respect. Kindness breeds kindness.

Honor breeds honor. If you smile and say "good morning" to someone, they will typically do the same thing back. (It's calling mirroring.) Don't be violent to yourself or others- both of those activities dishonor life. If you dishonor life, how can you appreciate your own life or other's people's lives? If you dishonor life, this can lead to disenfranchisement, ambivalence, and even suicidal thoughts. "If I don't think life needs to be honored, why would I honor my own life?" Disenfranchisement, ambivalence, and suicidal thoughts are not qualities of a person who is happy or satisfied in life. To honor life is to honor God. He created you and your neighbor, and you both are precious, and irreplaceable images of God himself.

The Secret Coping Skill: Honor Life

Honor life- in all forms. Whether you are nurturing a child, or taking care of an elder person in hospice care, or if you are taking care of an animal, or even if you are tending to a garden- honor life. Gardening is actually a long standing activity that has been found to decrease stress and anxiety, improve our mood general mood and self-esteem, and gardening has also been found to improve concentration! Honoring life through gardening is a wonderful activity to continue or to incorporate into your life. When we fail to do this simple act, living a happy lifestyle will become that much harder to acquire. And in the long run, honoring life is far easier and takes less effort and time than the alternative.

Aside from crimes of passion, being a criminal takes a lot of effort. You have to typically take time to plan out an attack, acquire weapons and learn how to use them. You have to find safe houses to hide from law enforcement or people who you have wronged. It is a very high stress life! In contrast to the criminal lifestyle, most people don't typically premeditate kindness! They just do it! Most people don't spend time or money on acquiring resources to take out an act of kindness! Honoring life costs you nothing, and it will reward you with great happiness.

~ "Blessed are the merciful, for they shall be shown mercy," Matthew 5: 7

Practical Ways of Applying "Honor-ing Life" as a Coping Skill

Honoring Life is a great way of living a happier life. Below is a list of practical was of applying this skill to your everyday life:

- Garden. This will help you increase your awareness of how hard it is to keep things alive and to appreciate how delicate and unique life is.
- Go to a garden. Go on nature walks and appreciate all the life you see. Go see and learn about plants like the Boojum tree or the Cactus. Those particular plants are truly incredible and a testament to life's persist-ence with survival.
- Adopt a pet, and take good care of it. Regarding ani-mals, take efforts to protect wildlife and nature at large. They are also a part of this universe.
- Volunteer in a program assisting the elderly, or new-borns. Hold their hands, and look them in the eyes. Connect with them and wish them well on their jour-neys. Both are at different ends of the life spectrum, and both are about to embark on something new and scary. The newborn is about to start on the journey of life, while the elderly is about to embark on their journey to death. Honor them for their courage.
- Don't be violent. Don't start fights, especially with people who are weaker than you.
- Assist a stranger in need. Be a good Samaritan. Give up your seat on the bus to someone who needs it more than you.
- Don't be wasteful. Eat your food! In a world that still struggles with hunger issues, eat the food you buy. If you have leftovers- eat them.
- Recycle.
- Greet the rising sun with a smile, and tell the moon "goodnight."

- Go to a zoo, a planetarium, an art museum, or a symphony. Allow yourself to be "wowed" by something. Don't be "too cool" to be impressed with things. Be honest enough with your feelings, to honor the thing that impressed you.

CHAPTER 6: Thou Shall Not Commit Adultery.

(The Secret: Balance)

T he words to this book came very easily to me. I wrote the first 40 pages of this book without a problem. All the subtle messages written between the lines of the other commandments came to me effortlessly. This chapter, however, did not. At first glance I thought it was about honesty - plain and simple. But (spoiler alert) commandment 8 is more about honesty, so you will have to wait until then to learn more about how honesty is a great life skill for increasing life satisfaction! In the meantime, let me take you on the abbreviated version of my journey of uncovering the secret to the 6th commandment.

Fidelity

One of my early theories about the coping skill for this commandment was that it was about the value of fidelity. Faithfulness, or fidelity is certainly a good thing to strive for! As a therapist I have certainly seen the ramifications of adultery on a relationship and the negative consequences of adultery on things like trust and self-esteem. Once infidelity is revealed, adultery is a very painful experience to live through. I had a friend call me the day after she walked in on her boyfriend of three years in bed with another woman. She was absolutely devastated.

To make matters worse, affairs typically do not last. Research has found that the person you had the life-altering relationship with will statistically not stick around for any length of time. By and large, affairs do not last. According to the website for Affairs Resource and Advice, "For every 100 people who have an affair, anywhere from 1-10 of them will marry their Affair Partner. Of those, statistics say that 75% will divorce within 5 years. So that means, MAYBE 1-3 out of 100 live "happily ever after" with their affair partner after leaving their spouse" (How Often Do Affair Partners End up Marrying and Happy, December 2012.) **In short, most adulterous affairs do not last.** So while the mistress/mister may not have been your long lost soul-mate, this does not mean that you threw away your previous relationship for no reason.

The mistress/mister could have been an escape, a fantasy, vengeance etc. The affair person is usually a symptom of a much bigger problem in the relationship, or your life. Either way, by and large, no matter how the affair starts, research has found that 75% of the time it **will** end. I typically see people in the aftermath of these adulterous relationships, and all parties are miserable. The adulterer feels crippling guilt and shame, the non-adulterous partner feels betrayed, embarrassed, angry; and even the mistresses have come to me reporting grief over the loss, embarrassment and shame for being "the home wrecker," or falling for the belief that the other person would leave their spouse, as well as guilt and shame for their actions.

I won't even get into the pain that any children go through if they become aware of these adult issues, but trust me, they too suffer from watching their parents at this time. I also won't even go into the psychological difficulties children have to go through with divorce due to these affairs, or the difficult transition it can be for blended families with various custody issues with multiple parents, or the more basic foundation of developing what a healthy, trusting romantic relationship should look like.

As a moral pillar, and as a goal for society to ideally function, this commandment seems pretty straight forward. *Don't physically or emotionally cheat on your partner.* Plain and simple. If you have found someone else that you like more than your partner- then tell your partner this news and go be with that other person. If you are married, talk to your spouse about your concerns and get counseling. A marriage is a sacrament, and it should not be abandoned lightly.

Why Fidelity if Not Enough

All of that being said, life is too short to not be with the person you love. But recognize that your choices will always come with its own unique set of consequences, and that nothing is going to reduce the amount of pain you will inflict on your family if you chose to cheat on your partner and get caught. Also recognize that there is no guarantee that this new partner is going to "be the one" either. Again, 75% of adulterous affairs fail. And let's not forget that 50% of marriages fail, too. The divorce rate in the United States has been hovering around 50% for decades, so clearly **fidelity is not enough to save marriages or our mental health.** People divorce their spouses for many reasons besides infidelity. So clearly then, fidelity is not enough to save marriages, and it is also not enough to keep people happy either. While the divorce rate in America has hovered around 50% for decades, the depression rates in the United States have been climbing. Research published in *The American Journal of Psychiatry* in 2013 found that major depression rates for American adults increased from 3.33% in 1991 to 7.06% in 2002.

If 50% of married folks are so unhappy in their first and subsequent marriages, to the point of divorcing that person, then that says to me that something besides fidelity is missing in their lives. Married people get divorced for many reasons, infidelity is only one of them. So living a faithful life or not, people still seem to be unhappy. What gives?

Loyalty

Similar to fidelity, I thought it could be about LOYALTY. To be loyal to someone or something does two very positive things for people. For one, it helps with our identity formation. In general, our "Identity Formation" is our basic inner concept of who we are, and where or how we fit into society. A healthy identity is a good sign of having a positive self-image/ self-esteem. To not have a healthy identity formation can leave us feeling "lost."

The second positive thing being loyal can do for us is that it is nice to think of ourselves as being a loyal person. It is considered a noble virtue to be "loyal." However, loyalty, much like fidelity, can be a burden, and it can also be used against us. Loyal people can do terrible things in the name of loyalty. I am sure that ISIS fighters consider themselves loyal soldiers. I'm sure gang members, and NAZIs considered themselves loyal people too. Acting in the name of loyalty can also have us placed in compromising situations which are very stress-inducing or downright scary. For a less extreme example, loyal and faithful employees could stay at their job for years- hating every second. But they stay out of a belief that they should be loyal to the company. Maybe a person stays with an abusive partner because they believe that loyalty is more important than their own happiness. While loyalty *can* help with our identity, it does not necessarily pave the road to life satisfaction. Clearly then, the secret lesson in this commandment is not about loyalty either!

The Real Secret Coping Skill: Balance

After much thought I believe I finally discovered the secret message in this commandment that had been eluding me. After thinking about it, I was embarrassed to see how obvious this skill was. I talk about this life skill every day. The skill in this commandment is not just about fidelity, and it's not just about honesty or loyalty. This commandment is about the importance of **BALANCE**, and it is warning us about the dangers of overindulgence. Gluttony, hedonism, greed, overindulgence, whatever you want to call it are all considered "bad" and are signs of an obvious lack of balance and discipline.

Overindulgence

Our society's' insatiable need for more more more is repulsive and life damaging. In 2016 The Center for Disease Control (CDC) reported that more than 1/3 of all Americans had been diagnosed as obese. In 2014 the CDC reported that 9.3% of Americans had diabetes. While that number may seem small, let me say it this way- that's 29.1 million people. That is the population of some countries!

Addiction

Addiction is another area where there is clear overindulgence. According to the Substance Abuse and Mental Health Services Administration's (SAMHSA) National Survey on Drug Use, "23.5 million persons aged 12 or older needed treatment for an illicit drug or alcohol abuse problem in 2009 (9.3 percent of persons aged 12 or older)."

More recently, in 2015 the National Institute of Health (NIH) estimated that at least 10% of adults in the United States have met criteria for drug use disorder at some point in their life.

How is this relevant to finding happiness? Similar to Elle Woods' comments about murder, most happy people don't shot heroin into their arm, or have bourbon for breakfast. That same NIH study from 2015 also stated, *"Similar to past research, the present study showed that people with drug use disorder were significantly more likely to have a broad range of psychiatric disorders, including mood, anxiety, post-traumatic stress and personality disorders. Individuals with drug use disorder in the past year were 1.3 times as likely to experience clinical depression, 1.6 times as likely to have post-traumatic stress disorder (PTSD) and 1.8 times as likely to have borderline personality disorder, when compared to people without drug use disorder. Drug use disorder was also linked to both alcohol and nicotine use disorder, with a three-fold increase in risk."* Clearly, the association between overindulgence and feeling unsatisfied in life is there.

Self-Control

One thing I do a lot in my practice is coping skill development. Having adequate coping skills is critical to living a happy, healthy life with well-managed stress levels. Everyone is going to go through disappointments, loss, rejection, grief, bad hair days, and so on. No one is making it through life without at least one day of stress or sorrow. That is why finding the right assortment of coping skills is so important.

I want you to think about coping skills as being on a continuum from immature coping skills to highly mature coping skills. (Not "bad" to "good", just "immature" to "mature.") For example, "denial" is considered a very *immature* coping skill. Saying something did not happen, when it did, may help with the momentary pain, but it will prevent you from moving beyond that moment. It's not "bad," though- just immature. Being in denial does not make you bad. The coping skill is not trying to misbehave. Its intention is to help you get through the moment. It just doesn't know better, or how to be better. Coping skills are thoughts or actions that are designed to help protect us from "overloading" from too much pain or stress, and ultimately to help us solve problems. Drinking alcohol and doing other drugs are another set of coping skills that I considered "immature." While drinking and doing drugs will work for the moment (much like denial), using substances will never let you conquer or solve the underlying problem.

All that being said, it is not the alcohol or drugs fault. And I'll even say that using alcohol or drugs isn't really the problem either. It is the overindulgence of them by adults, and the inappropriate use of them by minors. As a rule, I believe that a brain that is introduced to drugs and alcohol before that brain is fully formed is never a good idea. It's like shooting yourself in the foot before a marathon. That being said, there is nothing *wrong* with an adult having an alcoholic drink. Shoot, have two! Feeling stressed about an upcoming event: have a glass of wine, a beer, a cocktail. Just got fired: have a glass of wine, have a beer, a cocktail. Smoke a cigarette, take a moment to collect your thoughts and calm down. If you can do this without losing control, step outside of the world for a second, but know when it's time to come back. Know yourself well enough to know if you can or *cannot* do this.

If you cannot trust yourself to have one glass and stop, then don't start.

The Art of Balance

Food, shopping, alcohol or other drugs can all make a person feel better in the moment, but life is longer than a moment. And life also cannot be just about hedonism and feeling good in the moment. "Why not?" you ask. The problem with living in the moment and hedonism, is that it impairs growth. Whether we like it or not, the world keeps spinning, and we physically age. If we are still partying like a 20 year old when we are 40, something is off. If we are still going to the same bars, and laughing at the same jokes that we did in our youth, than that's another sign that something is off. That "off-ness" is a sign that while we were off overindulging, the world kept turning and left us behind. We neglected to balance our desire for "fun" with goals or responsibility. Growing up involves grasping the art of balancing comfort with taking care of the responsibilities and realities of this world.

Adultery: A Form of Overindulgence

Remember, a person in an adulterous affair, is a person who already has a sexual partner. Then this person goes outside of their relationship to have more sex with more people. A person can safely indulge in sex in a relationship with one person, but a person engaging in sex with multiple people is overindulging. This person's gluttony for more sex, more attention, more admiration from another person is the root of their compulsive behavior. A person does not even have to engage in a full blown sexual affair to have problems with overindulgence. Maybe one partner finds extra sexual experiences by watching porn, hiring prostitutes, or going to strip clubs. Or maybe one partner just goes on dates with outsiders, or flirts with others through online chats. All of these extramarital courting behaviors are examples of engaging in overindulgence, rather than being satisfied with what they already have. Our desire for MORE, and our culture's support of us "deserving more" is a disease that needs to be eradicated from this planet just like other horrible illnesses from history.

So much self-inflicted pain is caused by our unchained

impulses and craving. Addiction, sexually transmitted diseases, obesity, bankruptcy, gambling, materialism, hoarding, interpersonal conflicts, and divorce are just some of the problems I can think of offhand that are caused by a person's uncontrolled over-indulgences.

The Secret Coping Skill: Balance

As a therapist, I probably say this 100 times a week: "It's all about balance." Alcohol is fine, just know your limits. Food is necessary to survival, just be aware when you cross the line from healthy eating into overeating. Having stuff is fine, but be mindful of when you become too materialistic, start hoarding needless objects, or are going bankrupt. Sex is great, within the safety of a secure and trusting relationship. Sex can also be criminal and traumatic with things like rape, human trafficking, and STDs. While it's not sexy or new, or easy, the truth is: it's all about balance. As I have said before, "if it's the hard thing to do, it is probably the right thing to do." Finding your own balance is definitely the right thing to do.

When you go off-balance in either direction you will find suffering. If you need a visual, I want you to envision a see-saw. On one end is a child wearing a shirt that says, "Overindulgence of needs." And on the other end is another child wearing a shirt that says "Ignoring of needs." Siding with either of those children will not bring you happiness. Finding your own balance between those two things is your obligation and your gift to yourself.

Similar to the see-saw visual, I often talk with my clients about the intimate relationship between **Sacrifice and Gain.** The more you sacrifice in your life, the more you gain, and the amount you gain in life is a reflection of how much you have sacrificed. It's opposite has a similar fate. The less you sacrifice the less you gain, and if you refuse to sacrifice anything, you will gain nothing. This correlation came to me after saying to a client, *"those who refuse to sacrifice anything will inevitably lose everything."* Sacrifice is key for happiness, while overindulgence and compulsion is key for stagnation and misery.

You Can't Have it All...But You Can Be Happy

You like drinking, having a family, and having a job? You can have it all- if you can balance not drinking in excess, or working in excess, or spending all your time with your family. You love shopping and acquiring stuff? That's great! Make enough money to afford it, and remember to release yourself of the things that no longer bring you joy so you don't end up hoarding. If you only like wearing the latest and greatest fashions, then there is no reason to keep a closet full of clothes you aren't wearing anymore. You like having a safe committed intimate relationship? Great! This is going to involve ending any outside relationships that involve flirting or receiving emotional and sexual enjoyment from others outside of your committed relationship. Like eating donuts? Fine, I hope you also enjoy exercise, and some other healthier food options.

Balance Balance Balance. Since it is literally impossible to "have your cake and eat it too," the only real way of finding satisfaction in life is to start with living a balanced life.

I appreciate that most don't like to hear that a person cannot have it all. So in case you skipped over the part, I will say it again, "You can't have it all." You just can't. I tell my toddler this all the time! The other day I had to tell him that he could not watch *Dora the Explorer* and *Finding Nemo* at the same time. Trust me, I'm his mom, I would have loved to make this possible for him. But it was not possible, and so I had to help him choose between the two in the moment. My three year old can balance his desires, and so can you! Wanting it all is natural, it's just impossible to have or sustain for any significant period of time. It's like what the Rolling Stones said, *"You can't always get what you want. But when you try sometimes, you might find, you get what you need."* Astute words from an iconic band. They were right. We cannot always get what we want, but when we try (to live a balanced life), we can get what we need.

Icarus

There is a great Greek myth that illustrates this point about balance beautifully. The moral of the story is about importance of balance, while warning us to learn to appreciate our human limitations. It is the story of Icarus, the son of a great engineer of the time. In short, Icarus's father built him a pair of beautiful wax wings that allowed him to fly. All Icarus had to do to enjoy this superhuman ability was to not fly to close to the sun or too low to the sea. Icarus did not listen to his father and he flew too close to the sun, which caused the wings to melt and fall apart. Icarus then went crashing into the sea and died. Needless to say, this story is a tragedy. However, it is teaching us that when you can find balance in your life, and accept the factors that are present in that moment, it is only then that a person can begin to find peace. Oddly enough, and so eloquently depicted in the story of Icarus, it is only when you find balance in your mortal life that you can fly like a God!

Practical Ways of Applying "Balance" as a Coping Skill

Learning how to apply Balance into your life is a great way of living a happier life. Below is a list of practical was of applying this skill to your everyday life:

- Save money for a specific goal. Whether the money would be for an object or a trip. Rather than putting it all on a credit card, save the money and pay for the thing you want fully. It will take more time, thus increasing the odds of living a more balanced life with discipline and pleasure.
- Go on that vacation! I know so many hard working people that never take trips! Some of them have weeks of vacation stored up they still don't go. Work isn't going anymore. If you are a self-identified workaholic, please try to incorporate a healthy work-life balance back into your life. The world, and probably your family misses you.
- Exercise in moderation by listening to your body. Start with 30 minutes a day of active exercise. Go

ahead and take the stairs instead of the elevator. Or park further away in order to force yourself to take a walk. In our modern age we sit so much. Get up and move to balance out our sedentary lifestyle.

- Eat when you are hungry. Not because the clock tells you to.
- Eat a healthy diet with a full range of foods. It doesn't have to be vegetables all the time. But it can't be pizza every night either. Balance our sweets with our proteins and grains and veggies!
- Get good sleep, every night.
- Signs of imbalance will come up on your bank account, your weight, mood swings, interpersonal problems, and or general fatigue.

CHAPTER 7: Thou Shall Not Steal.

(The Secret: Selflessness)

"**D**on't Steal." Again, another seemingly obvious rule that needs to be followed in order for society to function. While it may be obvious to some, this commandment may not necessarily highlight how not stealing could not only keep you from being incarcerated, but how it could also increase your happiness with life as well.

I hope you are sitting down for this chapter because this next secret for happiness hidden within this commandment may be shocking for some. Consider yourselves all trigger warned: The underlying message to this commandant is to not only be respectful towards each other and to not steal- but even more so- it is telling you to Stop-Being-Selfish. Stop being selfish, and stop being self-centered, (and yes there is a difference) and both need to stop. Right. Now.

Definitions

To clarify, a "selfish" person is a person who immediately thinks about themselves, and how to manipulate the situation to best benefit themselves. These people tend to be a little more socially savvy, sneaky, and manipulative.

"Self Centered" people are a little less emotionally evolved, a little less socially savvy, and as a result of this, they have a tendency to exclusively think about how a situation personally effects them, without thinking about how it effects other people. Here is an example to demonstrate the differences between these two types of people. A *selfish* person will hear about an upcoming promotion and say to him or herself, "*I need that promotion, I don't care that "Linda" has been here longer and has three kids to feed. I want to go to Europe this summer and I need that boost in pay. How can I prove that I deserve that promotion more than anyone else?*"

A selfish person's behavior is direct and well thought out. A *self-centered* person is a little less culpable. A self-centered person would also hear about the promotion and say, "*Oh man I need that promotion! How can I prove that I deserve that promotion?*" The self-centered person is not burdened by all the extra thoughts about other people, and what they are doing, or what they deserve.

Notice how both display the same line of thinking, but that the latter has no thoughts of other people, or ideas of screwing over others. Another major difference between these two types of people is that a *self-centered* person could be easily talked into generosity/philanthropy to others when it is brought to their attention. Someone could tell a self-centered person, "*Hey, Linda has been here longer than you, and she has three kids to feed. She has also been working her tail off just like you- but it's her turn.*" A self-centered person could hear this and genuinely say, "*Oh my gosh, I didn't realize that! Linda is a work horse, she deserves a promotion too. May the best employee win!*" A selfish person could be told the same thing and not care.

Material Objects Will Not Bring You Happiness

Whether you are selfish or self-centered person your behavior needs to change if you want to be happy. Ironically, thinking about just what you want all the time, and "acquiring" what you want all the time will not make you happy.

One reason is because research has found over and over again that possessions will not give you happiness. Experiences will keep you far happier than any "thing" will (Van Boven & Gilovich, 2003; Van Boven, 2005.) Experiences provide you with happy memories, growth opportunities, and typically more opportunities to be more social with others. Studies have found that when research participants are even asked to think about paying for a vacation, or paying for an item, that the people thinking about a vacation produce more positive feelings than the people thinking about buying an item (Van Boven, 2005).

Why Material Objects Don't Work

For example, when you work hard and buy an object- say it's a fancy watch, you may genuinely really value and treasure that watch. But your watch doesn't care about you. You are in a one way relationship with that watch, and one was relationships are doomed for failure. As much as it shines on your wrist, and ticks away, it would also gladly shine and tick on anyone else's wrist. I am sure there are readers out there who have been in one-way love relationships before, and remember how unfulfilling it was to be in those relationships. This is no different.

This is not to say that some objects cannot be sentimental or special. Some objects can acquire special significance. Maybe the watch was a gift from our dying grandfather, or we bought it with our first paycheck from our first job out of college. When objects start being seen as extensions of a loved ones, or are big memory triggers to happy or significant times, then yes it can become "special." This type of emotional value increases the object's overall value. But overall, when there is not any special meaning behind an object. Nice things are just nice things, and the excitement and pleasure that we got from them initially will eventually run out. They will become old, dusty, rusty, and eventually obsolete. As the old saying goes, "the things that truly bring us happiness in life, are rarely ever *things* at all."

Our memories and experiences on the other hand will never betray us like our possessions do. That memory of our child's first steps, or that vacation to Rome, or our wedding day will always be loved and cherished. I have spoken to divorced people who still share about how amazing their wedding day was, even knowing in the present that the marriage didn't work out. Our cherished experiences, which become our cherished memories will never become obsolete to us. They will forever remain a source of happiness and joy for us to turn to when we are feeling low. Cherish your experiences of joy and happiness. They are as precious and valuable to your spirit, as diamonds are to your bank account.

The Dangers of Stealing

When you steal something, you are acting in an incredibly selfish ("Me-Centric") way. Stealing not only decreases the item's value, but it also decreases your value to society. No one likes thieves. Why are you making yourself unlikeable? Making yourself unlikeable will not make you happier.

Stealing hinders a person's abilities to respect and value others, and if you want to be happy, you will have to find a way to respect and value others. Research comes out time and time again about one particular variable that positively contributes to a happy life. That variable is "good relationships." Healthy, stable, long term relationships are a major contributing factor to happiness in our life. To achieve and maintain a healthy stable relationship with someone, you will need to respect them and value them as a person. Stealing from them is not a way to show them respect, or that you value them. Some even say that stealing, particularly shoplifting, is a "victimless crime." But it isn't really. The store owner is impacted, and other law bidding citizens are impacted as well. Because of the known variable of shoplifting, store owners are now inflating an item's price to make up for speculated losses. So because of predicted shoplifting, store owners are punishing the good citizen by making you pay more. That doesn't sound like a victimless crime does it?

Stealing also interferes with a person's basic concept of money and hard work. For example, if you did steal that gold watch, the value of it then is $0. That is how much you paid for it. If you stole that gold watch to give it to someone, you are essentially saying that you care about them enough to make the sacrifice to spend $0 on them. It's also a huge slap in the face to the gold miners who worked long dark hours to collect the gold for that watch. It's a slap in the face to the goldsmith and jeweler who designed and forged the watch. It's a slap in the face to the store owner, who was maybe hoping to sell that watch for $500, rather than getting $0 for it. But you wanted it for free... Newsflash: you aren't that special. If you were that special, someone would have bought that watch for you, or you would have bought it yourself.

"But I wanted it!" I am hearing somewhere out there. And to that person I say "Great! It's great to want things and to know what you want. You now know what your goal is. Now map out a way to achieve that goal legitimately.

"But work is hard, and finding work is hard too!" And to that I say, "If it's the hard thing to do, it's probably the right thing to do."

If you are unwilling to work towards your goals, then you are typically either unworthy of the goal you set, or you actually don't really want the goal you say you want. If you are unwilling to spend your own resources on something you say you want, then by stealing it you are showing how much you think it's worth- $0. Ergo, you think you are worthy of spending $0 on yourself. If you can think about the Cognitive Triangle feedback loop that lives within your mind and body, I challenge you to think about how you think spending $0 on themselves (the *action*) can make a person *feel* and *think* about themselves.

When your antisocial actions of stealing occur, that action is going to make you *think* that you are only worthy of spending $0 on yourself, which is going to make you *feel* like you are worth $0. When people are in good moods they say things like, "Wow, I feel like million bucks!" No one who feels good about themselves ever says things like, "Man, I feel cheap" or "Man, I feel like a whole lot of nothing today." The things we do and the things we say strongly impact our mood. Be cautious and conscientious about what you do and say in order to exert your power and control over your mood.

Know What You Want

If you are unwilling to compromise or work on, or make any sacrifices, then your actions tell me that you prefer to spend your resources of time, money or general sacrifice on yourself- rather than another person. This is selfishness. You are consciously choosing yourself over anyone or anything else. And since people cannot steal things like *good relationships*, or *intelligence*, the only way to acquire these goals are through hard work, sacrifice, and change. Sacrifice is the ultimate currency you need to acquire worthwhile goals. Tangible goals of objects, and nontangible goals like happiness and good relationships will require sacrifice on your end. If you are unwilling to spend your any currency to buy a healthy relationship, then I would say you don't want a healthy relationship. Going back to the previously discussed Sacrifice-Gain Model, if you want to gain anything in life, you will have to sacrifice something to get it.

Here is one personal example of saying that you want something when maybe you don't really want it. This is a silly, and even slightly vain personal goal that highlights this idea of my Sacrifice/ Gain Model. I have been saying for years that I want to be a size 2 one day before I die. Yet I refuse to give up sugar, carbs, alcohol, cakepops, cheese, tacos or increase my exercise regimen. Typically I get to about a size 6 and tell myself, "This is good enough," and then I continue on with my life. While I still tell myself that I have a dream of being skinny one day, I am not doing anything for that dream to happen. Wants and dreams don't get things done- actions get things done. If I was my own client, I would tell myself that perhaps I am unworthy of the goal, or that it isn't really what I want, if I am unwilling to make any sacrifices to gain said goal. I would therefore also ask myself if the Size 2 is really what I want, or do I want to eat cakepops... and the answer so far has always been cakepops!

Another less silly example is when people come to me and say that they want to be in a meaningful romantic relationship. They say that, but then are unwilling to sacrifice their vulnerability, their time, or money, and defenses enough to gain and build a meaningful relationship. Everybody wants the instant gratification of sex and attention where the only sacrifice they make is typically taking their clothes off long enough to gain the sex and attention. Don't fool yourself with the lie of "I sacrificed my body and boundaries- so why can't I gain a meaningful romantic relationship?" This is a distorted take on the Sacrifice-Gain Model. The strategy of sleeping with someone right off the bat doesn't work for the same reason prostitutes and their buyers don't have meaningful relationships. It was fun, and it was easy, and everybody got something out of it. There was no real sacrifice. If the intent was to try to "force" a relationship, then it was more so manipulative than a true sacrifice. Also, the Sacrifice-Gain Model cannot be fooled. Even when individuals sleep with someone before they are ready, something I hear a lot is "well I thought he would be more interested in me if I slept with him. So that's why I did it." This thought, while understandable, is self-serving and demonstrates that you were trying to manipulate the other person into liking you more. Therefore the sacrifice was not genuine. You attempted to use your body to scam the person into liking you before they even know if they like you or not. You used your body and sex to try to skip over the necessary requirements of vulnerability and respect in meaningful relationships. You tried to cheat the system, which never works. Therefore when you "sacrifice" your body and have sex too early in a relationship, all you will gain from it is the short-term satisfaction of another person's body and sex.

Meaningful romantic relationships take the sacrifice of vulnerability and the allotment of trust to a possibly untrustworthy person. Meaningful romantic relationships require the sacrifice of your vulnerability and defenses to share meaningful information about yourself, your background and your beliefs to (again) a possibly untrustworthy person. It also takes the sacrifice of listening and learning about another person. A meaningful romantic relationship takes the sacrifice of your time away from yourself and your life, and to give it to someone else. Because of this you may have to eat at a restaurant you have never been before, or it might mean you go to an event that sounds boring to you. Your sacrifice in these areas, will gain you that meaningful romantic relationship.

The truly important things in life that can make life wonderful are what I call the "intangibles." Intangibles are things like love, a great family, good health, integrity, respect, and friendships. None of these things can be purchased or stolen, they all take hard work, sacrifice, and selflessness to acquire. These are the things that will truly add to your life, and they are also the things in the world that even the most talented of thieves cannot steal from you. And it is for that reason that robbers continue to rob, and thieves continue to thieve. Because no matter how much they steal, it is never really what they want, and it never fills the void of loneliness in their hearts.

Original Sin

As discussed earlier in the Introduction, a deacon once told me that most people believe that the "Original Sin" was when Eve **stole** the "apple" from the Tree of Knowledge. While this is the superficial or obvious sin, the action of taking the fruit has a deeper sin. And that sin is selfishness. When Eve stole that apple, her actions spoke very loudly that, 1.) I am going to do what **I want** because I am so special that I am above the agreed upon rules of society. And 2.) I am so special that **I want** to know what God knows. Notice how the words, "I want" have been bolded in those two sentences.

Dr. Freud

I want, I want I want, are the words of what Freud called our "Id." Freud suggested that our personality is divided into three constantly competing components. These three components are the Id, Ego and Superego. The Superego pulls for our best self. This is the piece that holds our morality, principles, values, as well as criticism to try to "keep us in line." The Superego wants you to always do the right thing.

The Id is the superego's opposite. It pulls for you to choose the hedonistic, instinctual, selfish option every time. The Ego's job is therefore to balance the two opposing views and try to be a rational, reasonable human being. The Id is where selfishness lives. The Id could also be blamed for all our antisocial behaviors, as well as why we don't ever reach some of our goals. The Id is the short-term thinker and only thinks about what it wants right now. Eve wanted the apple, and she wanted it right then. Without regard to the rules, or the potential consequences, she acted in selfishness and stole the apple. That one selfish act was her downfall. Like Eve, it still only takes one selfish act to ruin our likes

The Dangers of Selfishness

Eve's selfish choice also negatively impacted the lives of others, and again to this day it only takes one selfish act to negatively impact the lives of others. Think about the selfish person who drives drunk and kills an innocent person. Think about the jay walker who causes an accident, all so that he doesn't have to walk all the way to the crosswalk. Think about that sick person who gets on a plane because he wants to get home and doesn't care about infecting all those other passengers. We are not that different or removed from Eve. Our selfish behaviors can have disastrously negative consequences for others whom we have never even met. We can all learn from Eve's mistake. We can all be better.

The Secret Coping Skill: Selflessness

When the world can replace selfishness with selflessness, the world will know peace. And everybody in the world will know peace as well. Selflessness highlights a person's abilities for empathy and compassion. Two amazing qualities to have. If we are empathic, we can have a greater ability for selflessness, because we can start to visualize ourselves in the same situation, thus making it more personal, and easier to be kind and compassionate. The Bible encourages it's readers to harness our abilities for compassion and selflessness. When we can do these things, we can get ourselves back on the road to leading a happier life. 1 Corinthians 10:24 "Try to do what is good for others, not just what is good for yourselves." On the idea of selflessness, St. Thomas Aquinas wrote prolifically on the importance of Charity. He believed that Charity was so important for a person's salvation that he named it a Virtue, and believed that performing acts of charity provides our souls opportunities to be "virtuous and perfect." Furthermore, on the topic of Charity he said these words, "charity truly leads to happiness, since eternal blessedness is promised only to those who have charity. For all other things are insufficient without charity" (J.P. Torrel, 1985.)

Charity in Action

While most religions clearly value charity work, the field of psychology has scientifically demonstrated the value of volunteerism on a person's mood. Time and time again, researchers have shown that volunteerism and other prosocial behaviors have resulted in only positive effects on a person. Johnson & Post (2017) recently published their research on volunteerism saying that "helping others in meaningful ways generally results in a happier, healthier, resilient, and even longer life spans for the giver." Other researchers say similar things such as, "participation in volunteerism has great potential in helping individuals reach their desired goals such as improved self-esteem, sense of purpose, social connectedness, happiness, quality of life and community inclusion" (Miller et al., 2005) As a therapist, I frequently encourage my patients to incorporate volunteerism into their schedules to help themselves increase their self-esteem, increase their mood, and as an avenue of making new friends and fighting the dangers of isolation.

I had a great friend in high school who struggled with depression. While we were in high school she explained that her symptoms were "manageable." She had a great relationship with her siblings, and her parents, and she was popular in school and was a highly esteemed Varsity athlete. She said that things went downhill for her when she went off to college. For the first time she was now managing her symptoms alone, away from the support of her family, her popularity no longer had any clout, and her skills as a high school athlete were no longer praised. Long story short, after a scary first semester of over drinking and over drugging, her parents brought her home and put her into counseling. One thing her counselor encouraged her to start doing was volunteering. My friend said that she had always really loved animals, so she choose to volunteer at her local animal shelter. This move no doubt saved her life. She ended up caring so much about those animals that she even curbed her drinking and partying behaviors so that she would be in shape enough to work at the shelter the next day. She also started bringing animals home to Foster. The animals gave her life an increased sense of purpose, meaning, and love. Today my friend is doing great. She ended up going back to college and graduating. She still fosters animals from her local shelter, and she has many great friends who love her. Depression is still something she has to manage, and she tells me that whenever she feels like her depression is starting to creep in, she goes back to her local shelter and volunteers. While charity may have been designed to save or help the lives of the more unfortunate, charity can also save or help the life of the charitable person. Charity is a win-win all around. All it asks of you is selflessness.

While charity is clearly a free, non-medicated approach to improving a person's overall happiness and life satisfaction, Johnson & Post (2017) went as far as saying that, "the time has come for health care professionals to prescribe and recommend such behaviors (volunteerism) at sustainable levels generally in the range of two hours per week." That to me is an amazing sign of progress! In a time when "pill popping" is an epidemic, imagine how much good could be brought to our communities if folks were prescribed volunteerism rather than a pill. That is progress.

Practical Ways of Applying "Selflessness" as a Coping Skill
Learning how to apply Selflessness into your life is a great way of living a happier life. Below is a list of practical was of applying this skill to your everyday life:

- Increase your compassion towards others. Before you act, try to think about how your actions are going to affect other people. Ask yourself how you would feel if you were the other person.
- Listen to Others. The next time you are with someone. Try to listen to them without interrupting them. Let them speak. Don't try to compare their issues or problems with your own. Don't do this, "Oh yeah that sounds hard. But listen to this my day has been worse!" Don't be in competition with them. Don't try to solve their problem. Just listen.
- Be Patient with others. Just grin and bear it! Again, try to think how you would want to be treated, or how you would like someone else to treat one of your loved ones.
- Practice Charity/ Donate your time or money to a cause. Or clothes, or an old car, or furniture. There is so much need out there. Find ways to give.
- Stop speeding and compromising everyone else's safety! I know I have said this one before- but Speeding, running red lights, and stop signs is lethal and a huge sign of selfishness. No one needs to die because you are late for the airport. The next time you get behind the wheel remember that others out there are counting on you to drive safety. Arrive Alive, and let others arrive to their destinations safely too.
- Give up your seat on the bus to someone who needs it more.
- Volunteer. It doesn't matter for what. Just volunteer.

CHAPTER 8: Thou Shall Not Bear False Witness.

(The Secret: Honesty)

I f you don't know what "bearing false witness" means, it means to lie. This commandment is commanding its followers to not lie. The secret to a happy life from this Commandment is very straight forward: **Honesty**. If you want to live a happy life, you need to live an honest life.

As a therapist, I have advised people struggling with anxiety and depression to practice **honesty** at every chance they get. I have found that, by and large, the honest objective truth tends to create a far more hospitable world than our over dramatic distorted fantasy world that our mood created. Dr. Lisa Najavits, a groundbreaking clinician and researcher for the treatment of substance abuse and post-traumatic stress, compared the practice of honesty to a "spiritual sense of acceptance" (Najavits, 2002.) In her **Seeking Safety** treatment manual, she also discusses the "psychic cost of dishonesty," which she described as, "(dishonesty) alienates (ourselves) from others and perpetuates the idea that something about (ourselves) is unacceptable and must be hidden" (Najavits, 2002.)

If you are lying, cheating, or even being deceptive about something, you are doing those things in an attempt to not get caught. If you don't want to be seen doing something, or you do not want to get caught having done something, you probably feel that way because whatever it is you are trying to hide is somehow considered morally or socially deviant. I doubt there are many people out there who are worrying about getting caught for something if they aren't doing anything dishonest or deceptive! Ergo, it seems safe and reasonable to conclude that living an honest life is a way of living a healthier, happier lifestyle. Simply put, the hidden message in this commandment is about the power of honesty.

Sometimes, worrying about the *possible* outcome of something is worse than the outcome itself. I remember one time I accidentally ran into my parent's garage door, from the inside of the garage, and busted it off its hinges. I was 22 years old, with no "fix-it-yourself" skills, and I was terrified! As soon as I got to work and I started calling multiple different businesses to fix it, but all the quotes were well beyond my financial ability to afford to fix it on my own. I decided to bite the bullet, and I called my dad and told him the awful truth. After the initial, "WHAT!" and my rambling of apologies, he started laughing at me so hard that he couldn't even talk! He said, "You actually 'Austin Powers-ed' the car out of the garage through the other garage door?! How long did that take you!?!"

Clearly, my hours of anxiety and worry and efforts to cover up the accident, were worse than the actual feared stimulus of telling my parents about what I had done. In that example, notice how I was only suffering when I was trying to be dishonest. When we lie or deceive others, we are doing so because we feel shame about the truth. In that above example, I was embarrassed about my mistake. I was rushing, thinking about too many things, and forgot to open the garage door before I backed up! I felt stupid, embarrassed, and ashamed.

Compounding the shame to our mistakes and our deceptions, comes the stress of the lie getting discovered. Because if that were to happen, not only did we do something wrong or stupid, but now we are also a liar, who was disrespecting the listener who we told the lie to in the first place! Now we have to come to the objective truth that we did something wrong that we felt shameful about, and we also have to face the facts that we additionally became a disrespectful liar. The downward spiral just keeps getting worse! *"Oh what a tangled web we web when trying to deceive."* While being honest would not solve all the world's problems, it would certainly help with decreasing individual anxiety and reducing our levels of shame.

Honesty typically brings with it a sense of certainty, while lying brings uncertainty in regards to consequences. For example, if we were all robots who were hard wired to be honest, we would still be capable of doing amoral things such as cheating, stealing and killing- but we would not have to live with the uncertainty of wondering, "What's going to happen IF I get caught?!" We would know the consequences and we would accept them much easier than we can now. Partially because our robot selves would have at least never started lying to themselves or others about the indiscretion in the first place.

Live in the Present

As a general rule, living in the present is a great way to live, and a great skill to cultivate. Anxiety lives in the future, while we live in the present. And since humans cannot predict the future, we can forever be wondering, worrying, and crying over the unknown future. The best and most time efficient way of handling a lot of internal stress is BEING HONEST.

Some examples of honesty could look like this:

1.) "You broke your mother's favorite flower vase." Rather than waiting for her to find out, or lie to her and say you don't know what happened, try honesty. Choosing deception and lies is a permanent addition to your life. From here on out, you will have to live with the stress and shame from keeping the deception and lies alive. 20 years from now, when Grandma brings up that she wanted to will you her favorite vase that broke, you will be reminded of the deception and lie you told her. "Too bad the dog knocked it over!" will be the line you will have to remember forever. Remembering the lie and carrying the deception is a burden that never goes away. Choosing honesty nips this in the butt.

2.) "You told your sister you can go to her birthday party knowing that it's also your daughter's first piano recital and thus you have no intentions of going to the birthday party." As a therapist I see this kind of situation a lot. This inability of saying "no" off the bat causes a lot of unnecessary stress in our lives. Some call it a difficulty with saying "no," I call it a difficultly with honesty. When you know you cannot do something, but tell people you can do it, this is dishonesty. Then you have to work through the fear and anxiety of trying to explain why you won't be able to make the event, as well as why you thought you could make it in the first place! If this problem sounds familiar to you, some therapists would talk to you about your difficulties with assertion, or that it's a confidence problem, or it's because you are such a nice person because you feel discomfort with letting people down, and these therapy conversations would certainly be helpful and the guidance would be kind and gentle. Here is the "no kid gloves" response to this "lack of confidence" problem: try honesty. Honesty will nip future problems and discomforts in the butt right away, and everyone is back on the same page! "Are you coming to my birthday party on Friday?"- Oh no I can't! I'm so sorry but it's my daughter's piano recital! We will go celebrate together another time."- Boom, problem solved.

The Secret Coping Skill: Honesty

So be honest. Live an honest life and I can almost guarantee you will experience a reduction of stress. Honesty can work its magic before problems even come up, and can sometimes prevent problems and a-moral behavior in the first place. So many of our bad behaviors, and so many bad events are born from miscommunications between each other, or our own distorted perspective on something we heard or saw. So take the time to explain yourself and your feelings- they matter. Take the time to tell the other person that you don't understand something. Make them explain it or themselves to you until you understand. If you are feeling unappreciated/unloved by your spouse- say so. It will take courage, and even a dose of vulnerability, but try. Try to correct a problem before it gets too overwhelming to solve. (Remember: If it's hard, it' probably the right thing to do.) Live a proactive life with honesty, rather than a reactive life with deception. You won't regret it.

In addition to the dangers of lying, and the benefits that honesty can do for our mental health, I believe that this commandment is also warning people about the dangers of words and gossip and all the other ways we humans have for deceiving each other. Ever heard of the phrase *The Pen is mightier than the sword*?" This is a metaphor designed to highlight that language can be more harmful than physical acts. When we engage in lying and or gossip about someone else, we are engaging in an invisible war against our own truth, our own identity, as well as the other person's reputation.

Ancient Wisdom

Socrates once advised his students to ask themselves three things before they speak. Socrates said to ask themselves if the information is "true," "kind" and "necessary." Socrates advised them to only continue speaking if the answer to all three of those questions was "yes."

However, just because something is "true" does not mean that you now have the moral freedom or obligation to go spreading the news to everyone. Just because "Julie" gained 30lbs over the summer does not mean that you are not obligated to go tell everyone in the office about Julie's weight gain. Do not be so arrogant to believe that you have been chosen as *the one* to enlighten everyone about this news. Don't even pretend to lie about your desire to be honest by saying, "well it's true. Sorry if the truth hurts!" Regarding poor Julie, your intention was not to be honest. Your intentions were to gossip about the misfortune of another person, and to be the first one on the block to talk about a new topic. Your intentions were to gain attention, it had nothing to do with any desire to being a more honest person.

If we could live an honest life, without deception, and without gossip, we would all feel better about ourselves. It would also free up our time to talk and share about more important, higher level, global things. Remember: *"Great people talk about ideas. Average people talk about things. Small people talk about other people"*- (Author Unknown.) Be Great. Be modest, but stay Honest.

Practical Ways of Applying "Honesty" as a Coping Skill

Learning how to apply Honesty into your life is a great way of living a happier life. Below is a list of practical was of applying this skill to your everyday life:

- Be up front as soon as possible. As soon as you recognize a problem, or a situation that you are afraid of, approach it with honesty rather than with avoidance. For example, if your boss asks, "Can you work on Saturday?" and you can't, tell them you can't! Don't say "yes" only to call out on Saturday with some sort of lie that you are sick. If you can't work on Saturday, tell the person you can't work on Saturday.
- Be courageous and vulnerable with the hard truth. And praise yourself for this courage. It takes guts and maturity to be honest. So when you do practice honesty, give yourself credit for it. You just did something that a lot of people struggle with. Go you!
- Remember that you would want to be told the truth, and not lied to.
- Think of honesty as a way of solving a problem. It's a tool, not something scary. Sometimes we need a hammer to fix a problem, and sometimes we need honesty. It is that simple.
- Own Up. If you do lie, try to correct it as soon as possible. Don't just sit in wallow in guilt. Don't go to church and confess. Correct it. Don't allow the person

to continue believing the lie. Apologize. It takes a real grown-up to apologize and own up to our mistakes. So correct the dishonesty with honesty, and move forward in truth, rather than with lies and deception.

CHAPTER 9: Thou Shall Not Covet Thy Neighbor's Wife.

(The Secret: Healthy Boundaries)

"Covet" is defined in the dictionary as "to yearn for, to possess, or to have something." As you the reader have probably figured out by now, I enjoy breaking down words to their simplest form. I find that when I do this, expressing ourselves becomes very clear- and that much more powerful. I think it is also a helpful way of reminding us about what we are really communicating. This is why in general I encourage my clients to reduce/eliminate their use of dramatic and absolute language. While dramatic words can be great for creating emphasis, or to be funny, hyperbole and absolutes, typically take away from the truthfulness of the message. In an attempt to take up back to the topic at hand, just remember this: Words matter, choose wisely. Communicating well is critical for any society to function. Now back to Coveting!

Now that we understand what the word "covet" really means, let's re-read this 9th commandment with its simpler language: "Thou shall not *want to possess* thy neighbor's wife." When I read this commandment this way, I get a suddenly different vibe. This message is ripe with both obviousness, and abuse. I leaves a very bad taste in my mouth. It is sort of like when someone tells you not to do something that you would never dream of doing in the first place. It would be as if someone came around the corner and said, "*and don't poison the stray animals.*" It makes my mind say, "*Well obviously! Who in their right mind would do that anyways? That would be so messed up to do! No one needs to tell others not to do that. It's insulting that you even felt the need to tell me not to do that!*" Well ladies and gentlemen, I hate to be the barer of bad news, but there are some very unhealthy people out there that do need to hear obvious things like the above messages because otherwise the behaviors would occur. It's the same with drinking and driving laws. Obviously drinking alcohol and driving is a bad, dangerous, idiotic thing to do, but people still do it. Hence there are now laws banning the behavior. People still do it, but at least there are harsh consequences in place for this unacceptable behavior. That being said, while it may seem obvious to you that "not wanting to possess your neighbor's wife," is a very good life rule to follow- it is not as obvious to some.

Outside of the negative impact of things like envy, (which will be further discussed in Chapter 10) a healthy person should not want to possess another person. A person is a person, not a lamp. You can own a lamp. You can own several lamps. You can start a lamp store. You cannot and should not ever own or want to own a person. The moral and ethical and psychological impact of even the idea of owning a person is beyond the purposes of this book. But in short, you cannot, and should not want to, own another human being. Nevertheless wanting another human being who is already in a relationship with someone else. But this commandment is not just about the sins of trying to steal another person's partner. It is much deeper than that.

The hidden coping skill that I see in this commandment it about practicing and respecting basis **healthy boundaries**. Respecting healthy boundaries for ourselves, and respecting healthy boundaries of others. The fact that this commandment was written thousands of years ago, suggests that humans have had problems exercising healthy boundaries for thousands of years! People with healthy boundaries do not own people, nor do they want to own other people. Healthy people likewise do not want to be, or allow themselves to be owned or controlled by other people. Healthy people seek to own things like animals, land, and well, other things! People with healthy boundaries seek out things like, love, respect, trust, intimacy, and friendships. They do not seek out to own or possess another individual. It is not right, and it is also not healthy.

Dangers of Unhealthy Boundaries

When people do not have healthy boundaries, several very unfortunate things can happen. On the most basic level, people with poor boundaries typically have lower self-esteem, and they have a knack for putting themselves in danger. They don't know how to ask for help when they need it, and don't know how to assert themselves well. They also tend to allow others to violate their own boundaries, and people with low self-esteem also tend to violate other people's boundaries as well.

There are two main types of boundaries that will be discussed in this chapter. The first one are Physical Boundaries. Physical boundary violations would be things like burglary, assault, stalking, voyeurism, exhibitionism, sexual harassment, hitting, punching, kicking or other forms of physical abuse like that. While the above are the more obvious forms of physical boundary violations, physical boundary violations could also be done through acts of littering, vandalism, or reading through someone else's diary, emails or texts.

The second type of boundaries are Psychological boundaries, or Emotional boundaries. While not as visible, boundary violations here can cause very serious problems. Psychological boundaries consist of our own internal rules of conduct for ourselves. While violating a psychological boundary would not land a person in jail, these are the types of violations that land a person in shame spirals. Psychological boundaries outline and put structure on our own personal integrity, or dignity. Examples of this would be, "*I would never sleep with a married man,*" and then you do. Or, "*I would never stay with an abusive partner,*" and then you do. Or even, "I always stop to help the needy," and you don't.

The above examples demonstrated how we can violate our own psychological boundaries, but psychological boundaries can also be violated by others. Emotional and verbal abuse are the most obvious examples that come to mind. Withholding love is a common one. If you know that you have a partner that craves words of love and adoration, and you purposely stop saying "I love you," that is a subtle form of passive aggressive abuse. Or telling people that they are never going to achieve their dreams and aspirations because they are too stupid, lazy, or unlikeable, that is emotional abuse too. All are examples of boundary violations.

Objectification & Co-Dependency

As we spiral down into the deeper circles of unhealthy boundaries, we tend to find two horrible monsters. One is called Objectification, and the other Co-Dependency. Both are dangerous in their own way, but they sometimes overlap themselves in some situations. Objectification is sometimes alone, and sometimes with Co-Dependency, but Co-Dependency is always with a partner. Co-dependency does not like to be alone. If you ever get a sense that one of these monsters is looming near you, my advice is to run!

What is Objectification? It is defined as "the action of degrading someone to the status of an object." It is part of the "dehumanizing" process. Its purpose is to extract your humanity, so that the extractor no longer has to treat you like a human being. It is the Objectifier's way of dismissing the other person's boundaries. To a selfish person, treating others as human beings is very inconvenient. When dealing with another human being you need to take into account their needs, their desires, their feelings, their hopes, and dreams. Human beings need things like water, food, sleep, bathroom breaks, clothes, affection, respect etc. When dealing with another human being you also have to practice respectful communication and you have to consider what they may want from the interaction. All very inconvenient for very selfish people. Therefore Objectifiers try to objectify other people as a way of bypassing this inconvenience (and any guilt for their behavior.) Because if the Objectifier got it in their mind that you are no longer human, then he/she is under no obligation of treating you like a human.

As I mentioned before, Objectification can either be spotted alone or with Co-Dependency. Example of Objectification *alone* is when there are disrespectful superficial encounters with strangers or when there is a tolerated uneven power dynamic-like a boss or a supervisor in the workplace. These bosses are the bosses that ask you to work on Saturdays, don't approve leave, and bombard you with extra responsibilities. They don't care when you are sick, or take into consideration your needs. You are nothing more to them than a worker Bee to them. They also don't care if you quit. You are nothing special to them, and they will find a replacement "you." Just like they would find a replacement for a broken lamp.

Objectification can also be seen in the family setting when there are clear power differentials. This would often then be called Child Abuse or Intimate Partner Violence (IPV). Huge examples of boundary violations. Abusers here treat their "loved ones" like objects and dismiss their needs. Being treated this way often makes people feel unappreciated, depressed, like they don't matter, unloved and often fearful. The objectified can often feel angry and resentful, and build up hatred for their abuser. While there are not co-dependency issues in child abuse situations, most cases of IPV situations demonstrate classic Co-Dependency patterns. While the victims of objectification may hate, and often do hate their objectifiers, they are definitively the non-participating victim in the relationship. They are not doing anything to promote this unhealthy relationship, and if given an out, many leave if they can. Or the victims at least dream of leaving. This is why children in child abuse situations are not considered "co-dependent." True Co-Dependency is found when both people in a relationship are active participants in a very unhealthy relationship that demonstrates no form of respectful boundaries.

Co-Dependence is spotted through a persistent pattern of seriously unhealthy and dangerous behaviors found in relationships and attachment styles. These relationships have extremely poor boundaries, to the point that there is almost no boundary between the two individuals. Individuals with Co-dependence issues "need" to be in relationships, and will suffer through abuse and neglect to keep a relationship alive. Co-Dependent individuals suffer with extremely low self-esteem, and rely on their partners for a sense of both identity and approval. Due to their extreme desire to maintain relationships, and their fear of being alone, when a relationship starts to fall apart, they tend to fall apart too. They may become more impulsive, illogical, short-sighted, "animalistic," desperate, and even violent. Violent towards others or themselves.

As I mentioned before, Co-Dependence hates being alone, and is more often than not spotted with another person. A main feature of Co-Dependence is that the partner here is considered an active participant maintaining the unhealthy behavior of Co-dependency! This is an essential difference between Co-Dependency and Objectification. While the Objectified person does not participate in the de-humanizing process, the partner in the Co-Dependence dance does. Sometimes this behavior is referred to as "enabling." To give a real world example of a Co-dependent relationship, one person will get labeled some judgmental term like "the co-dependent" or "the crazy one," or the "addict." While the partner who ACTIVELY STAYS WITH THIS PERSON, is labeled the "poor victim." Mental health experts highlight how healthy individuals with healthy boundaries would never stay in these Co-Dependent relationships. The Co-Dependent would burn out any healthy person's patience and emotional stability. A healthy person would not tolerate the constant distrust, and neediness of the Co-dependent. Therefore it begs the question- "who stays with these Co-dependents?" The answer, other unhealthy people who find purpose in being "a rescuer," "the nurturer," or even "the martyr." The partners find such purpose in their powerful roles with their unhealthy partners, that they will put up with the fights, and tears and violence, for the chances of maintaining the relationship. Obviously, this is a very unhealthy relationship marred with litter to no boundary or separation between the concepts of "them" and "I."

Recovery from Co-dependence is a hard road but it is possible. While there are no defined steps for ending these unhealthy patterns, the first step to most recovery is identifying it as a true pattern for themselves and wanting to change. Building self-esteem will be essential, as well as learning coping tools and self-soothing tools to tolerate uncomfortable feelings of loneliness in early recovery. With better self-esteem it is will easier to identify abusive behavior from others, and to see that it is "ok" to refuse this type of treatment. Learning that it is "ok" to say yes or no to something/someone is another way of enforcing Healthy Boundaries! It is another way of saying, "I am worthy enough to be safe. I am worthy enough to be treated well. I am worth enough to be loved, and I am worthy enough to be happy."

The Secret Coping Skill: Healthy Boundaries

Everything is better with healthy boundaries. Healthy boundaries are primarily enforced through saying "yes" or "no." If you struggle with telling people "no," this is a life skill that you need to cultivate. In my clinical practice I say this phrase often, "Learning how to say *no*, is something you need to *know*." Likewise, healthy boundaries also consist of learning how to say "yes." Remember, boundaries are set in place for the ultimate goal of keeping you safe, and feeling respected. We cannot be expected to be able to know everything, do everything, and be in multiple places at once. I guarantee that at some time in your life you will need help from someone. Learning to say "yes" and accept help from others is a lifesaving skill. It is equally as important a lifesaving skill as learning to say "no." You need both.

To highlight the value of saying "yes" I would like to share with you a true story. In my late 20's I had a friend who lived with a roommate. Let's call my friend "Erin," and the roommate "Sarah." One night my friends and I decided to go out to the bars. Erin showed up without Sarah, which was very uncommon. Erin and Sarah were best friends, they almost never went anywhere without each other. Because of this uncommon event I asked Erin where Sarah was. Erin said that Sarah wasn't feeling well and wanted to stay home. This seemed like a totally understandable thing, so I didn't question it. The next day we all went to a late brunch and Sarah still didn't join. Erin again said that Sarah wasn't feeling well. Three days later Sarah was picked up by an ambulance from their apartment and taken to a hospital where she stayed for two days. Doctors reported that she almost died. Sarah had suffered some type of severe urinary tract infection with a subsequent uterine polyp burst. She was severely dehydrated and had lost a lot of blood. While Erin had been checking on Sarah throughout those few days, Sarah kept saying "I'm fine! I think I am just having a bad period." On that third day when Erin came in to check on her she found Sarah unconscious, and that was when she called the paramedics. While this may seem like a serious example, not asking for help, almost cost Sarah her life.

More common and less serious examples of saying "yes" are for things like homework help, learning how to read, asking help with directions, help with changing a tire, or saying "yes" when your boss asks you if you need a break. Becoming comfortable with saying "yes" is just as important as being comfortable with saying "no" to protect your boundaries. You can think of boundaries like your own personal fence or wall around you. Sometimes it is in our best interest to say "yes" to people entering our Kingdom, and sometimes it is in our best interest to say "no" to other people. It's not mean. It's healthy. And happiness will never be found in the boundless chaos and confusion of the Dominion of Unhealthy Boundaries. Happiness will only be found in the peaceful, predictable, and safe Kingdom of Healthy Boundaries.

When a person can exercise healthy boundaries, life becomes easier. Our anxieties get reduced, conflicts reduce, and feelings of resentment start to dissolve. Why? Because of the stability and predictability that boundaries bring. Due to this increase sense of stability and predictability, our confidence can grow and we thus feel more capable of accurately expressing our thoughts and our needs to others. Setting healthy boundaries are good for both you, and everyone else you encounter. When a person has boundaries, it's like carrying around their own personal "life manual." The rules are in place, you know them, you reinforce them as needed, and slowly but surely everyone else comes to respect (or at least accept) your rules of conduct. Everyone gets their needs met, and expectations are managed. Healthy boundaries set the stage for a peaceful life to happen. Healthy boundaries ensure that you respect yourself, that you respect others, and that others respect you. With healthy boundaries, everybody wins.

Practical Ways of Applying "Boundaries" as a Coping Skill

Learning how to apply Boundaries into your life is a critical piece of living both a safe life, and a happy life. Below is a list of practical was of applying this skill to your everyday life:

- Know what your personal preferences for boundary are- or what you want them to be. If you don't want to go to a particular side of town, don't go. And don't let others push you into going. If you don't want someone to touch you, don't allow them to touch you. If you don't want to talk to someone about a trauma, you don't have to talk to them about it.
- Make your boundaries known. Let your desired boundaries be crystal clear to everyone. Let there be no confusion about what you like and don't like. This can help with expectation management for your friends, and it can help "train" others about how we want to be treated.
- Have no tolerance for boundary violators. Yourself included! If you break your own rules, others will infer that you don't really care about your rules, and they will in turn violate your boundaries as well. "Monkey see, monkey do!" Something else to remember, setting up boundaries is just the first part. Once those boundaries are in place, you will have to inforce them and protect them! "Eternal vigilance is the price of liberty!- Leonard Courtney. Throughout your life, friends and enemies alike will try to violate your boundaries. It is on you to reinforce and protect

them.

- Learn how to say "yes" and "no." These two little words are two of the main ways we communicate to others about where our boundaries are. Our safety and self-respect lie in knowing how to weld these words.
- Tell yourself daily that you are worthy of Safety and Respect.
- Respect other people's boundaries. Even when you are unhappy with the outcome. When you respect someone else's boundaries it increases your chances of them respecting yours.

CHAPTER 10: Thou Shall Not Covet Thy Neighbor's Things.
(The Secret: Gratitude)

Commandment 10 also functions off of the word of "coveting." As discussed in the previous chapter, while yearning to possess someone is always a bad thing, this commandment forces as to ask the question, "what is so wrong with wanting to possess things?" Well for starters, it becomes a problem when we want things that we cannot have, such as other people's things. If something is possessed by someone already, we therefore cannot possess it. To possess something that belongs to someone else would conflict with Commandment #7 (Thou Shalt Not Steal. Please re-read that section if needed!)

Wanting something that someone else already owns breeds envy. Envy is a very unhealthy place to stay for too long. Envy, or jealousy, can lead to anger, greed, hatred, entitlement, resentfulness, and selfishness. To quote the great Jedi Master Yoda, "*Anger, fear, aggression... the dark side are they. Once you start down the dark path, forever will it dominate your destiny.*"

There is a reason envy is considered one of the seven deadly sins according to the Catholic Church. In addition to Envy being a Deadly sin against the Catholic faith, it is also a "deadly sin" against our own ability to be happy. Since this is the last chapter, I am going to give it to you straight. Here it is plain and simple: A person cannot be happy if they are jealous. It's just not possible.

If you are a jealous person, you are an unhappy person. Why? One reason is because it keeps you from having a genuine relationship with the person or people you are jealous of. If you are jealous- you are wanting something that you do not currently have. This is also true for individuals who are jealous in relationships. If you are a jealous partner, this suggests that you struggle with trust issues, which makes it substantially more difficult to have a happy, honest, stable, and genuine relationship with someone else. Again, jealous people, envious people, are unhappy people. If you are focused on the things other people have, or get caught up on thoughts about how "unfair" the world is, you are blinding yourself from seeing all the gifts and opportunities that you do possess!

Life Is Not Fair

Before we go any further, we need to review a very serious concept. While nobody wants to say it, or hear it, learning this life lesson of not coveting can be summed up in three little words:

1.) Life
2.) Isn't
3.) Fair.

And yes, I know what you are saying right now, "*Duh doc, I know that. Everybody knows that.*" But I question how much everyone really believes this phrase. While the words are easy to say and we all "*know that*," I don't think people really comprehend the gravity of what those three words really mean.

So much pain and suffering in our lives comes from our perspective, what we believe, and the *expectations* that we have for ourselves, others and the future. All of those expectations set us up for opportunities to either feel happy and appreciative, or upset and victimized. We can either set ourselves up for failure, or success; it's all up to us.

One principle that always needs to be factored into all situations is this axiom that "Life Isn't Fair." Life does not care if you planned an outdoor wedding. If rain is going to fall, it is going to fall. Life does not care if you are going on a first date with your crush and you grow a pimple on your nose. It doesn't care about any of your plans or hopes and dreams. Life does not care if you achieve your dreams, or if you fall short. The world will keep turning in spite of the outcome. The world is quickly labeled as cold and uncaring when things do not go our way. Then we often scream into the sky about unfair life is. The scary reality here is that no one can argue this. Life is unfair, but that ok. It is "ok" because life never promised us that it would be fair.

Here is the thing- to believe that life is expected to be "fair" implies that we also believe that the world, universe, or God functions under a subscribed set of agreed upon rules and laws. Rules and laws are created from entities such as societies, governments, and cultures. Rules can also be created by individuals which are called personal "rules," which serve to help a person go about their daily life with some sort of code of conduct. Society's rules are things like laws: "Don't drive over the speed limit." Cultural rules are the "shoulds." An example of cultural rules are things like, "Women should cover their hair and shoulders in church." Personal rules are things like, "I don't use public restrooms." No matter where our rules and laws come from, we know that all the rules can be broken. We know that the universe does not follow our rules. Outside of the laws of math and physics, there are no rules or laws, or personal plans that the universe follows.

It's Physics

The world does not care about our Bill of Rights, or the 10 Commandments, or the Geneva Convention, or the Magna Carta. If the world *did* care about those things, we would not be physically *able* to steal, kill, or be jealous. It would be physically impossible. Let me give you an example. In video games, certain characters can only do certain things that the game allows. Allowed behaviors have been programmed into the system. Typical behaviors that are allowed are actions like "run," "jump," and "shot." These commands were programmed into the video game and allow the character to perform them. Any non-programmed behaviors cannot happen. This is why when you were playing Super Mario Brothers, you were able to run and jump, but you weren't able to get Mario to water the flowers, sing, or take a nap.

But we aren't Mario. We have not been programmed to only perform a few set of motions. We are humans, with free will. For better or for worse, everyone has free will, and we live in a universe that has not been programmed to only do a few set of actions. The universe does not follow man-made rules. The only rules that the universe follows are things like gravity and the seemingly forward march of time.

One rule that the universe and Earth seem to follow is the phenomenon of Gravity. For example, every time you release your pen, it will fall. That being said, if you ever do release your pen and it does NOT fall, THEN you can say that the universe is not being fair. EXPECTING gravity to work every time, is something that the world has demonstrated is a law, and therefore something you can expect and count on. For gravity to suddenly stop working, *that* would be "unfair." But to say that "life isn't fair" because you didn't get into your number one college, or you didn't get the job, or because you and your husband are divorcing? I would say "no." It certainly is sad, upsetting, and life altering. Maybe you had expectations of moving to the school, or getting your dream job, or that you and your partner would be together forever. Maybe now you need to pivot and change your plans. All these examples would be sad and frustrating, and maybe even a little scary to live through. But unfair? Did the universe promise these things to you? No. Is your marriage a part of the laws of physics? No. Your divorce is possible because in our world, divorce is possible. A gravity defying object: impossible & unfair. The sun never setting: impossible and unfair. The sun not setting and gravity not working are two examples of things that have been deemed impossible and unfair due to the thousands of years of human's experience with consistent gravity and sun setting.

(**Caveat:** Just because I am highlighting that all human actions are possible, I am not saying those actions are moral or right. Horrible tragedies occur and terrible people do terrible things. Horrible, unforgivable atrocities occur daily. Trust me, I'm a therapist, I've heard the worst, most heartbreaking events and stories. Just so we are clear, just because something is physically possible, I am not implying that the behavior is "ok," acceptable, or fair. I am just saying the world will not stop to care. People should still care. Society, the government, our communities, our families, friends, neighbors should care. We should do our best to prevent horrible behaviors as much as possible. And we should all do our best to nurture a person who is suffering from a tragedy. We should all care about each other's heartbreaks. But when we expect the WORLD to care about our heartbreaks, we allow ourselves to feel abandoned and hopeless.)

Here is the main problem with not fully embracing the idea of "Life Isn't Fair." To complain about how unfair life is implies that you expect it to be fair. And to expect it to be fair, implies that you believe life functions by some sort of agreed upon rules between you and the universe. And to believe in that, implies that you believe that the world is a just and predictable place. The world is many things, but "just and predictable" it is not. There are millions of examples of this axiom throughout the world and throughout history. Some animals are super-fast, or strong, or huge, or smart, while some animals well- aren't. Is that just? Is that fair?

Some of us are born into rich families and some of us are born into poor families. Some of us are born with brilliant minds that can solve complex math problems, or can learn 16 languages, and some of us cannot, and are instead born with brain disorders that leave us struggling with our native tongue, and basic math. That doesn't seem very fair does it? No it's not fair. Because Life isn't fair. But did Life promise you otherwise?

People want things to be fair and equal, because fairness and equality makes us feel that rules are in place to keep us safe and protected. *"If things are fair and equal I can just always follow the rules and I will be ok."* If there are no rules, then what will keep us from being hurt, used, or victimized? Here is the honest answer: Nothing. No government or written laws will keep you from ever being hurt, used or victimized. I know this revelation can be terrifying, but it is true. The world is an unpredictable, unfair place with no safety rails. Lying to yourself that it is a fair/

safe place will only leave you more vulnerable and naive. The faster you accept this truth, the better. People who do not want to accept this truth typically suffer with feelings of prolonged anger due to their felt injustice, and their identification as being a victim. They also tend to struggle with profound anxiety due to their conflicted views on that the world should be a predictable place with followed rules, while knowing it is not a predictable place that follows rules. This idea that Life Isn't Fair is extremely distressing for those who value control.

The Power of Acceptance

I know this is a tough pill to swallow. I recommend taking it with a big glass of ACCEPTANCE. Acceptance is a beautiful thing. It releases us from our struggles, and typically our pride. This is one reason why I suspect people don't like it. If you can AC-CEPT that life isn't fair, you can release yourself from expecting it to be fair, and then you can release yourself from the burden of fighting a relentless truth of this world.

Now that you have been enlightened, you can stop whining and coveting all the things you do not have. After you have done this, you can fully start appreciating the things you do have. You don't yell at the sun for being bright, or at the rain for being wet do you? Then why yell at life for being unfair? The sun is bright, the rain is wet, and life is unfair. So wear sunglasses, buy an umbrella, and embrace that the world owes you nothing except for gravity and the other laws of physics. It is only when we have learned how to accept what is, that we can stop fighting for fantasies that will never be. Once we can do this, we can start being grateful for things, and then we can be happy. Learning how to be grateful will be one of the most important skill you ever learn. For I believe that a person can never be happy without gratitude.

The Secret Coping Skill: Gratitude

This brings us to the final and arguably most critical skill for happiness I pulled from the Commandments. The art of gratitude. Gratitude has been defined as, "the experience of appreciating the positive aspects in life," (Alkozei, A., Smith, R., & Killgore, W., 2017.) More simply, it has been considered a way of showing our appreciation or thankfulness for something or someone. Research has found that feelings of gratitude have been associated with increased subjective wellbeing (Alkozei, A., Smith, R., & Killgore, W., 2017; Crystal, C, 2017.) One researcher even concluded that "gratitude" is one of four factors necessary for obtaining happiness (Maeno, T., 2017.)

Additional research has concluded that "Gratitude is considered an important source of human strength in achieving and maintaining good mental health" (Jans-Blake et al, 2017.) Other psychological researchers have determined that implementing gratitude exercises can lead to increases in reported levels of happiness (Dickens, L. 2017.) I could go on, but I think you get the point. There is a lot of research out there confirming this idea that practicing gratitude will increase your levels of happiness. While a lot of the research on gratitude is new, obviously the practice of gratitude is very old. Ironically, it seems that science is finally turning to our past, and our old culturally congruent ways, to increase our subjective experience of life and happiness. Since practicing acts of gratitude are clearly an "old school" thing to do, it begs the question "how did we get so lost?"

How Did We Get So Lost?

Frankly, I blame reality TV and our worship of celebrity for the scarcity of gratitude in the modern American life. I've observed that most reality TV shows like to show the most dramatic scenes with polarized emotions, while the people in the shows are also living a luxurious lifestyle. Lots of yelling, lots of swearing, lots of threats, lots of sex. Exotic vacations, beautiful clothes, and lots of options for fine leather handbags. I guess it's considered boring to watch nice people who model gratitude?

Reality TV and celebrity magazines highlight an unrealistic, dramatic, ostentatious lifestyle. We all know the headlines, "Rapper Blah Blah just crashed new Ferrari! Bought new one next day!" "Football Star and model wife just purchase 10 acre property in Malibu for $20 million." Luxury handbags that cost thousands of dollars, million dollar trips to tropical places like the Maldives or Bali, parties on private jets and yachts. The American public is inundated with this type of material from all angles. The media praises these types of behaviors. It's everywhere.

What happens next is this unhealthy love and worship of our celebrities. Some people start to feel a (false) sense of connection between these actors and ourselves. We also connect to the imaginary person- the role that they play, and with the real actor. If "Mike" plays a sweetheart on TV, we the public assume that Mike is a sweetheart in real life. Some may even fantasize about how great it would be to date Mike and to be loved by Mike. Meanwhile, off screen Mike is a womanizer who drinks too much. But we love him anyways- because he is a sweetheart on TV. By ignoring the real "Mike the womanizer," in order to love the fantasy of "Mike the Sweetheart" the public has willingly made many moral sacrifices to believe the fantasy. The public has also then made unacceptable behaviors acceptable. In Mike's case, by dismissing or ignoring Mike's off-screen womanizing and drinking behaviors- they do not get corrected. When no one talks to Mike about his bad behaviors, Mike gets away with it. Now this is where an additionally problem comes to play in reality TV. If Mike was a reality TV star, his bad behavior would even be encouraged- because it increases rating and magazine sales! He would be reinforced to continue the bad behavior. Going back to the Sacrifice and Gain Model, our culture has sacrificed its morals and values, for cheap entertainment.

We overlook celebrities' ostentatious lifestyles, because on some level- we want that too. And that is understandable. So to rectify our desire for wanting (and not having) those ostentatious things, we vicariously get those things, and live those lives through the lives of these famous people we don't know. We then as a society made a silent agreement among ourselves that said it is now both acceptable and desirable to yearn for these outrageous things. In previous generations, desiring to "party on a yacht in Bali" would have been considered crazy and silly. Today, that is a totally acceptable life goal. Sadly, in our attempt to minimize our feelings of guilt for wanting these luxurious things, and any feelings of inadequacies for not having these things, many have decided to change their values in order to no longer feel guilty for their new materialistic goals. In other words, while a previous generation would have negatively judged someone for wanting a yacht, today's society is judging the yacht goal positively. This new society has approved these materialistic goals as worthwhile and good. We are now praising the celebrity lifestyle, rather than seeing it for its true nature: greed. The Bible warned us of the dangers of greed in 1 Timothy 6:10, "For the love of money is a root of all kinds of evil. Some people, eager for money, have wandered from the faith and pierced themselves with many griefs." I would like you to take a moment to think about how some celebrities have maybe pierced themselves with grief through their love of money. How you pierced yourself?

Look, I am a capitalist, I get it. You have the money, buy what you want. It's your money. Maybe you earned it, maybe you inherited it. Either way it is your money, and you have the right to spend it how you please. I really do mean this. But does a person really need a thousand dollar handbag? Does one person really need to own 10,000 pairs of shoes? While these seem more like moral- driven or value-driven questions, I hope they also inspire you to ask yourself the same question. And if the answer is "yes," explain to yourself why you need those things, and why the things you have are not good enough. Why do you want that thousand dollar handbag, and what would it mean to you?

I heard in a sermon once, "The things that make us happy are not things at all." If "things" made us happy than rich people would not be committing suicide, or going to therapy, or being addicted to any number of things. If "things" made people happy, then materialism would end after one shopping trip. "*I finally got that thousand dollar handbag! Now I will be happy!*" That never happens. Just because we see expensive and elaborate things everywhere, remember that those things, those people who buy them, they are the outlier- NOT YOU. And those happy smiles that are Botoxed onto their faces, will fade just like the Botox. Again, "the things that make us happy, are not things at all."

Practical Gratitude

Gratitude is the power to recognize the things we have and be appreciative that we have them. Gratitude is also the skill of recognizing that we do not have some things and are "ok" with it because we are ok exactly as we are right now with everything we do have. Don't have sunglasses? That's ok. Don't have a car? That's ok. Aren't athletic? That's ok. Missed the bus? That's ok. As you become more grateful for the things you have, it gradually becomes easier to be "ok" with not having other things. In other words, as you turn away from materialism and entitlement, you will open yourself up for more feelings of gratefulness and thus happiness.

Gratitude is more than a "silver-lining" exercise. Gratitude exercises are about actively searching for something positive and good to be thankful for and grateful about that either you, someone else, or luck/God/fate seemed to cause to happen. On the other hand, Silver lining searching is typically more about finding something positive in a bad situation. This is obviously still a great practice to do- but it's not exactly about gratitude. Gratitude searching goes beyond situations, and goes into your whole world experience. Gratitude is similar to silver-lining exercises, but they are deeper. Gratitude searching is also about exercising thankfulness to circumstances that were typically outside of your control. Like, "I am grateful that I met my wife at the bar that one night." Or, "I am so grateful that I wasn't in that lane where a car accident just happened." Finding ways to have gratitude with fate or the universe is one way of building up your belief that while the universe may be an unpredictable world, it's not out to get you.

I keep a poster up in my office that reads, "Life doesn't have to be perfect to be wonderful." It reminds me to be grateful for the way things are right now, and to not get caught up in what would make it "better" or "perfect." When we are "coveting" our neighbor's or friend's things, we are also disrespecting what we do have. "The Smiths across the street just got a new car! I want a new car!" If I was your therapist I would ask you what is wrong with your car? Millions of people in first-world countries don't have a car and you are complaining about your "old" car? Where is your gratitude for your car? Where is the appreciation for all the hard work it took you to buy that car in the first place? There is not gratitude in that example, and notice how there is also no happiness in that example either. When we find ourselves envious, try happiness for them, and then practice gratitude in ourselves. Example of this: "Wow the Smiths got a new car! Go them! Jerry really has been working hard."

Entitlement is the opposite of gratefulness. When we think that we are owed something, or entitled to something, we tend to dismiss our gratitude for what we do have. We take it for granted. We start seeing our entitlements as constants, rather than as fluctuating variables in our life. Constants are things like time running and gravity pulling things towards the ground. These constants are the only things the universe has promised us every day. Fluctuating variables are everything else, like your job, free education, free speech, or your legs working. These are the things the universe has not promised us. When we confuse the fluctuating variables with the constant variables, we start feeling ungrateful for the constants, and entitled to the fluctuating variables. The reality is that we need to start feeling entitled to the constants, and grateful for everything else.

When we feel entitled to something, we tend to get angry when it's gone, but do not feel grateful when it is present. This does not have to be the case though! We can still be grateful even when we are entitled to something- like freedom, or free education for children. We just have to remember to practice it, even for things we feel like we deserve. When we find ourselves envious, or angry, try gratitude for what we have. "Wow the Smiths got a new car! I know my car is a little older, but I am so grateful for my car and that I don't have to take the bus! Maybe in a few more years I too can buy a new car." I can hear the happiness in this example, can't you? When we can release ourselves from the chains of wanting and coveting things we don't have, we can open up our hearts for appreciation and gratitude for the things we do have. This is the key to happiness.

I encourage all my depressed patients to start a Gratitude Box. When I ask a patient to start a Gratitude Box, I ask them to write on a notecard something that they are grateful for at least five times a week. I ask them to date the card, and then put it inside their Gratitude Box. Then, at the end of the month, I ask them to open up their Gratitude Box and review all the cards. I love this exercise, and I have been doing it myself for years! After telling one of my clients about this idea, she said it sounded "nice" but that she didn't think she would be able to remember and follow through on it. So in order to help her out I agreed to keep one for her in my office. So every week that I saw here, I would write one thing down that she said happened, and then I put it in her box that I was keeping for her. Two months later, we had a session where she was crying and said, "why do only bad things every happen to me?" At this point I pulled out her Gratitude Box. I said, "I don't know if you remember this, but a while ago you asked me to keep a Gratitude Box for you. So I did, and here it is. Want to look through it with me?" She agreed, and we dumped out the box with eight weeks' worth of cards. Some of the cards said things like, "Had a great girls night at the Kareoke bar!" and "I got the promotion at work," "Had a great Movie Night with husband," and "I am grateful for my husband." She immediately began to cry again, but this time she smiled. She thanked me for keeping the Box for her, and for reminding her of all the good that she has in her life.

While the world is full of darkness and unpredictably, it is also full of unimaginable possibilities of hope, healing and happiness. Gratitude for what you already have is key on anyone's search for happiness. As we have already discussed, the things that make people happy are not really things at all. This begs the question, "what are things that make people happy?" There is much research on this question, but here are a few of the big hitters. Having a purpose and a meaning in your life. Waking up in the morning becomes much easier when you have a strong sense of purpose and meaning. Nietzsche wrote back in the 1800's that "he who has a why to live can bear almost any how." That "why" is your purpose.

Things That Will Give Us Happiness

Having strong, safe, and intimate relationships with others. Staying connected with others, verses being isolative and lonely is a critical factor in living a long and happy life. This is a conclusive findings from the Harvard Study of Adult Development that came out in 2002. That being said, my advice is to nurture your friendships and nurture your family and marriages. Try to release yourself from grudges and cultivate forgiveness for others. Our healthy relationships are precious and add great value to our lives and wellbeing. Do not neglect them. Spend time with your loved ones. Of "Deathbed Regrets," no one ever said, "I wish I hadn't spent so much time with my loved ones.

Travel, hike in nature, go to the ends of the Earth, and find opportunities to be "awed." Expose yourself to new people, new cultures, and the great places of the world. Spending your time and money on travel will be a much greater use of your resources then spending it on things. Research from Pchelin and Howell (2014) out of San Francisco State University found that people who spent money on experiences rather than materials items were happier and felt that their money was better spent. Traveling allows people to try new things, take a break from their typical lives, and they get the bonus of being able to reflect back on the good memories from their trip.

Outside of good relationships and traveling, other things that bring us happiness are things like fun, play, respect, intimacy, trust, and a feeling that we are striving towards our full potential. There are many great things in this world that can make a person feel happy. None of them are store bought items. That being said, whatever brings you true happiness, exercise gratitude for having it. Because a person could have a lot of the typical things that bring a person happiness, but if they are not grateful for it- they will miss their chance at happiness. Seize your happiness by practicing gratitude. It is more than likely within your reach.

Practical Ways of Applying "Gratitude" as a Coping Skill

As this chapter has discussed, learning how to apply Gratitude into your life is a critical piece of living both a happy life. Below is a list of practical was of practicing gratitude in your everyday life:

- Gratitude Box exercise. This was discussed at length in the "Practical Gratitude" Section. In short though, write down things you are grateful for at least three times a week and put those notes inside a box. It can be a shoebox, a Mason Jar, or an old coffee tin. Get creative and enjoy the exercise. After a month has passed, open up the Gratitude Box/Jar, and read all the notes!
- Gratitude Journal. Write down something daily that you were grateful for in that day.
- Say "thank you" as often as possible, to people, animals, plants, and the world. Get a box of "Thank you" cards and use them as much as possible. If you don't like to write- that is fine, but still say "Thank you" to others whenever you can. Don't let an opportunity to thank someone go by! My parents and I carpooled to work and school all through my high school years. And every my mom would point to this one tree on Quaker Ln and say, "Oh hi tree!" She just thought this one tree was especially beautiful, and she thanked it everyday for existing. At the time I thought it was a silly thing to do, but now that I am older, I think very highly of her for it. Imagine how much happier we would all be if we could be infused with such happiness from looking at an old beautiful tree.
- Donate your time, money, resources to a cause that you feel especially close to. If you feel grateful for having healthy children, donate to institutions like your local Children's hospital, St. Jude's or Shriners. If

you feel especially grateful to your past schools, donate your time and money to those schools. Find a way to give back.

- Recognize how luck/fortune/fate has positively impacted your life. This ties into the idea that "while life is not fair, it's not out to get you either." Give credit where credit is due. If you studied hard on that exam and earned an "A." Praise yourself for that. Thank yourself for that. To that same idea, thank life when it works in your favor. Maybe you found a great parking space right away. Maybe you picked a fast check-out lane at the grocery store, or maybe that car accident on the freeway happened behind you instead of in front of you. Or maybe you met your wife at that Farmer's Market that you normally never go to. The examples are endless. When you notice that life has favored you in some way, I encourage you to look up into the sky and simply say "thank you."

- Recognize something you are grateful for every day. If you don't want to do a gratitude box, or a gratitude journal, I encourage you to at least take a moment out of every day and remind yourself about something you are grateful for. It could be for your job, or your partner, your good health, that good parking space, or your vision. It could have been having the privilege of seeing that movie, or getting that pedicure. Be creative, and seek it out. Seek out gratitude. It will only make you happier.

CHAPTER 11: Conclusion

I hope you have enjoyed reading my thoughts about the secret lessons within the 10 Commandments. Before we move on, let us review the lessons that we have just learned. Believe in Something; Use Kind Language; Act on your Beliefs; Be Respectful; Honor Life; Find Balance; Be Selfless; Be Honest; Set Healthy Boundaries, and Exercise Gratitude. Following these coping skills will help you find greater satisfaction and happiness in your life, I guarantee it. These are all free to try, and are a non-medication based approaches to improving your life. What do you have to lose?

Nothing Changes if Nothing Changes

When I was at one of my first internship sites for my Master's degree, my supervisor had a poster on his wall with a simple yet powerful message: "Nothing Changes if Nothing Changes." This goes back to Newton's first laws of motion about how an object at rest tends to stay at rest, while an object in motion tends to stay in motion unless acted upon by an unbalanced force. More specifically, "*Objects resist accelerations. Objects don't like to accelerate. Left to themselves, objects don't speed up, don't slow down, and don't change direction. It requires an unbalanced force to change the velocity of an object.*" For this metaphor, we are the object, and we always resist change. Change is scary, change is the unknown, change is also saying goodbye to our old and predictable ways. Changing our lifestyle, and our perspectives, and behaviors is hard. But living an unhappy, depressed and anxious lifestyle is also hard. So what have you got to lose? Just because you may have fallen into an unhealthy lifestyle does not mean it has to stay that way. It just requires you to embrace change and to try living your life in a slightly different way. While it may sound tempting to some, you don't have to have an *"Eat, Pray, Love"* moment and quit your job and travel the world to find happiness. But you do have to make a change. If you want to change the velocity and direction of your life, you will need to embrace the "unbalanced force" coming at you. If you do not want to stay the same, you cannot remain the same. Nothing changes, if nothing changes.

God Wants Us to Be Happy

I had the pleasure once of having dinner with a modern day philosopher. In a discussion about God and fate, I made a comment about how I felt that God wants us to be happy. The philosopher's response was, "I don't think God gives a damn." The existence and the benevolence of an almighty God has been discussed for centuries, and it will not be solved today or anytime soon. As I said in the introduction, I am not a philosopher or a theologian, and I am not going to pretend to be. That being said, I do know what I believe, and I choose to believe that He did create us by design, and that He does want us to be happy. God and humans may have different ideas about what happiness means, but I still think He wants us to be happy. This is an unprovable thought, in either direction, and it is not hurting anyone. That thought makes me feel better, so I am going to continue thinking it.

If God "didn't give a damn" about our happiness, why is there such great mental health advice in the Bible about how to be happy? Why else would there be such great advice about establishing a civilized society, and parenting, and lessons about love, kindness, and forgiveness? And this is not just advice from one holy text. All the world religions' sacred texts hold wisdom and advice on living healthy and happy lives. If God, Allah, the creator, or the "Watchmaker" did not care about our happiness, why would a person or entity put forth the effort of writing down all this great advice about how to be happy?

"The Most Important Commandment"

I believe in all the coping skills that I pulled from the 10 commandments. If you want to improve your life and be happier, applying these skills will put you on the road to getting there. Much like dieting though, these skills must become a way of life, and not a "crash diet." I know you may be wondering if I have a "favorite" skill, or one that I think is "the best." I honestly do not. These "10 Secrets" are all strong, wonderful ways of improving the quality of your life. On this thought, I will conclude with a similar story from the Bible of when Jesus was challenged to name which of the 10 Commandments was the *most important* one. Here is what Jesus said:

"**Love** the Lord your God with all your heart and with all your soul and with all your mind. This is the first and greatest commandment. And the second is like it: **Love** your neighbor as yourself. All the Laws and the Prophets hang on these two commandments." (Matthew 22: 37-40, New International Bible.)

To me, it sounds like Jesus was saying that "Love" was the most important thing to do. Great advice. If you love your God (1st Commandment) then that means that you believe in something greater than yourself (the 1st Secret) and then, out of love you will act on your beliefs (Secret 3). And if you love your neighbor as yourself as Jesus encourages, then you will also follow the Commandments and all the Secrets. If you love your neighbor, you will not steal from them, or lie to them, or kill them, or disrespect them. If you love your neighbor as yourself, you would also want to practice balance in your life (Secret 6), with healthy boundaries (Secret 9), you would want to honor them and yourself (Secret 5), be honest with them and yourself (Secret 8), be respectful to them and yourself (Secret 4), be kind to them and yourself (Secret 2), and finally, you would want to act with selflessness (Secret 7) and gratitude (Secret 9/10) every day.

In order to make room for all the new secrets, or coping skills, in your life you may have to make some sacrifices. My typical suggestions are to start by releasing yourself from your pride. Let it go, it will only hold you back from happiness. We are our own worst enemies, and in my opinion our pride is our own personal weapon of mass destruction. There is no room for arrogance or pride on your journey to happiness. You can take your pride to your lonely grave with you but you cannot take it with you to find happiness. If you find it hard to swallow your pride or calm your arrogance, remember the tell-tale sign: "if it's the hard thing to do, then it's probably the right thing to do." At all times be kind. At all times, act with compassion. Act with kindness and compassion, and all the other secrets and coping skills will naturally start to happen, and before you know it- you will be happier.

I will conclude this literary journey with a quote from the great C.S. Lewis. In his book, **The Great Divorce**, he takes his readers through an imaginary bus ride that starts in Hell, where C.S. Lewis himself and other occupants of Hell catch a bus to take them up into Purgatory. In the book, C.S. Lewis is the narrator, and he watches damned souls attempt to leave Hell and enter Heaven. In the book, Heavenly spirits come down to Purgatory where the Heavenly Spirits try to talk the damned souls into giving up their pride, or anger so that they can enter into Heaven. C.S. Lewis watched many of the conversations between the damned souls and the Heavenly spirits, and this one that I am about to share is my favorite. The damned soul is bemoaning her existence and she says to the Heavenly Spirit, *"I wish I'd never been born... what are we born for?"* To which the Heavenly spirit replied,

" For infinite happiness' - said the Spirit. 'You can step out into it at any moment." (The Great Divorce, 1946, p.61)

I hope these words inspire you as they inspire me. Stop searching for happiness, and instead just step into happiness as Lewis's Heavenly Spirits suggest to. Step into happiness by using some or all of the coping skills that have been discussed in this book. Many people talk about happiness like it is an entity that "comes over" a person- like an ocean wave, or a raincloud. With these analogies, it makes the person look like the helpless victim to the desires and actions of the wave or cloud. We are more powerful than that. Rather than waiting for the wave to hit us, I say- jump into the wave. Step into the raincloud. Seize your power. Use these coping skills to help you seize your happiness. Happiness is not a secret, or something reserved for everyone else but you. Happiness is not a unicorn, it is real and it is waiting for you. It has been waiting for you all along. Be Kind. Be Grateful. Be Compassionate. **Be Happy**.

REFERENCES

Aces Too High. Aces Science 101. DOI: https://acestoohigh.com/aces-101/

Alkozei, Anna; Smith, Ryan; & Killgore, William, D.S., (2017.) Gratitude and subjective wellbeing: a proposal of two causal frameworks. Journal of Happiness Studies. Mar 23.

Aknin, Lara B., Van Bowen, Leaf, & Johnson-Graham, Laura, (2015). Abstract construals make the emotional rewards of pro-social behavior more salient. The journal of Positive Psychology, 10(5), 458-462.

American Psychiatric Association. (2013). *Diagnostic and statistical manual of mental   disorders* (5th Ed.). Washington, DC: Author.

Affairs Resource and Advice webpage. (2012). *How often do affairs partners end up marrying*, December 2012.
DOI: https://affairadvice.wordpress.com/2012/12/09/do-affairs-end-up-in-successful-relationships-13/

Catechism of the Catholic Church (1993.) Libreria Editrice Vaticana. DOI: http://www.vatican.va/archive/ENG0015/_INDEX.HTM

Catholic Bridge. (2017). Did Catholics Rewrite the 10 Commandments? DOI: http://www.catholicbridge.com/catholic/10_commandments.php

Child Welfare Information Gateway, (2013). Long-term Consequences of Child Abuse and Neglect, July 2013. DOI: https://www.childwelfare.gov/pubpdfs/long_term_consquences.pdf

Crystal, Chana D., (2017.) The roles of life satisfaction and materialistic values as mediators of appreciation. Dissertation. A Humanities and Social Sciences, Vol 78.

Dickens, L.R., (2017.) Using Gratitude to promote positive change: a series of meta-analyses investigating the effectiveness of gratitude interventions. Basic and Applied Social Psychology, 39(4) Jul 2017, 193-208.

Federal Bureau of Investigation. (2015). *Crimes in the US 2015.* www.fbi.gov/news;https://ucr.fbi.gov/crime-in-the-u.s/2015/crime-in-the-u.s.-2015/offenses-known-to-law-enforcement/murder

Green, M., & Elliott, M., (2010.) Religion, health and psychological well-being. Journal Of Religion and Health, June 2010, 49(2), 149-163.

Jans-Beken, L., Lataster, J., Peels, D., Lechner, L., & Jacobs, N., (2017.) Gratitude, psychopathology, and subjective wellbeing: results from a 7.5 month prospective general population study. Journal of Happiness studies, May 30, 2017.

Maeno, T. & Fukuda, S. (2017.) Four Factors of happiness as design parameters of a product/service. Emotional Engineering, Vol.5. pp 183-189. Charm, Switzerland: Springer International Publishing, viii, 197.

Miller, K., Schleien, S.J., Brooke, P., Frisoli, A.M., & Brookes III, W. (2005). Community For All: The therapeutic Recreation Practitioner's Role in Inclusive Volunteering. Therapeutic Recreation Journal, 39(1), 18-31.

Fang, X.; Brown, D. S.; Florence, C. S.; & Mercy, J. A. (2012.) The economic burden of child maltreatment in the united states and implications for prevention. Child Abuse and Neglect, 36(2) 156-165.

Hlavinka, Elizabeth, (2019.) Mass Shotting and Mental Illness. A teaching moment? Aug 8, 2019. www.medpagetoday.com

Johnson, S., Post, Steven G., (2017.) Rx, It's good to be good (G2BG) 2017 commentary: prescribing volunteerism for health, happiness, resilience and longevity. American Journal of Health Promotion, 31(2), march 2017, 163-172

Kocjanek, K., Murphy, S. L., Xu, J., Tejada-Vera, B., (2016.) Deaths: Final Report for 2014.

Lewis, C.S. (1946.) The Great Divorce. HarperCollins Publishing, New York, NY.

Matejkowski, J.C., Cullen, S.W., & Solomon, P.L., (2008.) Characteristics of persons with severe mental illness who have been incarcerated for murder. Journal of the American Academy of Psychiatry and the Law 36(1), 74-86.

Najavits, Lisa, M. (2002.) Seeking Safety: A treatment manual for PTSD and substance abuse. Gilford Press, New York, New York.

National Association for Mental Illness. (2017). Mental Health By the numbers. DOI: https://www.nami.org/Learn-More/Mental-Health-By-the-Numbers

National Fatherhood Initiative. (2016.) www.fatherhood.org. National Vital Statistics Report 65(4). Center for Disease Control. DOI: https://www.cdc.gov/nchs/fastats/homicide.htm
Pcheln, P. & Howell, R,T, (2014.) The hidden cost of value seeking: People do not accurately forecast the economic benefits of experiential purchases. The Journal of Positive Psychology, p. 322-334.

The Holy Bible: New International Version. Grand Rapids, MI: Zondervan, 1984.

Treatment Advocacy Center, June 2016.

Torrey, E.F., (2011.) The Association of Stigma with violence.

American Journal of Psychiatry, March, 168-325.

Van Boven, L., Gilovich, T. (2003). To do or to have? That is the question. American Journal of Personality and Social Psychology, 85(6), 1193-1202.

Van Boven, L. (2005.) Experientialism, materialism and the pursuit of happiness. Review of Gernal Psychology, 9(2), 132-142.

Waldinger, Robert (2016.) What makes a good life? Lessons from the longest study on happiness. TedTalk, Jaunary 25, 2016.

Wenar, C., & Kerig, P. (2006). *Developmental Psychopathology from infancy through adolescence* (5th ed.). Boston: McGraw Hill.

From a conference by **St. Thomas Aquinas** (*Opuscula*, In duo praecenta. Ed. J.P. Torrel, in Revue des Sc. Phil. Et Théol., 69, 1985, pp. 26-29. DOI: http://www.vatican.va/spirit/documents/spirit_20010116_thomas-aquinas_en.html

Made in the USA
Columbia, SC
30 January 2021